The Search for the
TASSILI FRESCOES

The Search for the

TASSILI

E. P. DUTTON & CO., INC.

NEW YORK   1959

FRESCOES

The story of the prehistoric
rock-paintings of the Sahara

HENRI LHOTE

Translated from the French by
ALAN HOUGHTON BRODRICK

Contents

MAPS

Translator's Preface

The whole of the author's text is given as it appears in the French version and the only additions are notes which the translator has furnished where they seem to be called for, as, for instance, to passages containing Arabic or Berber words.

Geographical proper names have been left in their French form when they refer to places in French-controlled territory. Proper names of persons have, however, been given in English transliteration—e.g. 'Jebrin' for the author's 'Djebrine'.

The word 'fresco'—representing the author's *fresque*—is to be understood as a colloquial term for 'rock-painting' or 'rupestral painting' and not as implying any real fresco technique.

A.H.B.

Foreword

A NEW page in the history of mankind was turned when the prehistoric grottoes of northern Spain and south-western France gave up the secret of their art treasures. The riches of Egypt and Mesopotamia were familiar, their history had been traced, and, confronted by the splendour of their architecture, their sculpture and their painting, we had long thought of them as the fount of all the arts, so varied were their techniques and so great their skill.

All such ideas on the origins of art were turned upside down by the deeply moving discoveries made in the caverns of Les Combarelles, Les Eyzies, La Mouthe and Altamira. Yet, the experts were at first doubtful that men so primitive, at such a low cultural level, and so limited in outlook, could have created works of art of such beauty, and their authenticity was suspect.

On this point the story of Altamira is instructive. It was the little daughter of the landowner who discovered the paintings and pointed them out to her father, Don Marcelino de Sautuola. The find caused a great sensation. Among the many visitors who came to look at the paintings was King Alfonso XII himself, but, when the owner conducted a party of the foremost scholars of the day to see them, he met with a charge of forgery. It appeared that some months before the discovery of the paintings he had had an artist as his guest. Nothing more was needed. This man must be the

painter of those famous wounded bison which were too modern in
style for the scientific bigwigs of the International Anthropological
Congress, held in Madrid, to accept them.

But, a few years later, the young Abbé Breuil, who was subse-
quently to attain world-wide fame as a prehistorian, visited the
cavern at Les Combarelles.[1] There on the walls were painted bison
—own brothers to those at Altamira. This time, since no one had
set foot in the cavern for a very long period (the way in had only
just come to light), forgery was out of the question. The evidence
had to be accepted.

Since then, the world has followed new discoveries in prehistoric
art with enthusiasm—Lascaux in 1940, and Rouffignac in 1956.

These rock-paintings are not confined to Cantabria, however.
Numbers are also found in eastern Spain—the Spanish Levant—
although these belong to another school, and are on the walls of
open rock-shelters, instead of inside caves. Again, in southern Africa
there are rock-paintings and engravings generally known under
the name of 'Bushman art'. The age of these works is uncertain,
especially as it is quite sure that the natives of southern Africa were
still painting rock-pictures only a comparatively short time ago.

The Sahara Desert (especially in the south of the Algerian
province of Oran) contains a great number of prehistoric rock-
engravings, but it was not until 1933 that it was revealed as an area
also rich in rock-paintings. These recent discoveries were all the
more exciting since we knew really very little about the great
desert's past, though there were signs to make us think the Sahara
might, in the past, have had a more abundant rainfall than at
present. Also stone artefacts, found here and there, proved the
existence, in far-off ages, of primitive populations and tribes.
Nevertheless, the information, such as it was, could only be

---

[1] I have left this reference to Combarelles as it stands in the text but there are no *paintings*
at this site, only engravings; maybe the Font de Gaume cavern is meant.

called fragmentary. Indeed, we knew nothing of the nature of those populations or of their origins.

For many years past I have devoted my life to scientific exploration of the Sahara. I have travelled all over it and I have studied it from the points of view of geography, ethnography and, above all, of archaeology.

The Saharan rock-paintings and engravings could not, of course, fail to excite my curiosity; so, after important discoveries of painted rocks had been made in the Tassili by a camel-corps officer, Lieutenant Brenans, I visited these sites with several specialists in Saharan geography and archaeology. Then came the 1939 war and the interruption of all my work. It was not until 1956 that I was able, with the encouragement and support of my revered teacher the Abbé Breuil, to organize a large expedition to copy the known paintings and explore systematically the Tassili massif.

The Tassili n'Ajjer (that is, the Tassili of the Ajjers) lies to the north-east of the Hoggar and to the east touches on the Fezzan. It is a sandstone plateau, difficult of access, and it forms the base or platform from which rise a considerable number of small, secondary massifs all heavily eroded. Through them you can make your way by means of narrow corridors overhung by cliffs, and of pillared areas that remind you of deserted cities. Today all this region is empty of life and an oppressive silence reigns. Once upon a time, however, the passages were streets lined with 'houses' since most of the cliffs are eroded at their bases and hollowed out sufficiently to provide natural homes for the early inhabitants of the region. These peoples have, it is true, long since disappeared, but they left hundreds of paintings on walls of their former dwellings.

Our expedition stayed sixteen months in all on the Tassili and during this time my fellow-workers and I made discovery after discovery, while, at the same time, we prepared, at each site, faithful copies of the frescoes.

Later I shall give some idea of what a gigantic undertaking this was amid a desert of stones and rocks and of our way of life in a land with no resources whatsoever and cursed with an inhuman climate. For the moment, it is enough to say we had a very hard time of it and that we should never have held out as long as we did had we not realized that we were doing something that was well worth while, since we were not only increasing knowledge of the Sahara's past but adding to the artistic inheritance of the world.

In fact what we saw among the maze of the Tassili rocks goes beyond the bounds of imagination. We copied hundreds upon hundreds of painted walls on which were depicted human and animal figures in their thousands. Some of the figures stood alone, others formed complex groupings. Sometimes the scenes were clear enough and related to everyday life or to the spiritual and religious existence of the different peoples which followed on, one after another, in sites that are now deserted save for the very few Tuareg who still haunt them. We were astounded by the diversity of styles and subjects and by the great number of overpaintings. Side by side with little figures, a very few inches high, we came across others of gigantic dimensions such as are unknown among prehistoric pictures elsewhere. Then again, there would be archers struggling for the possession of flocks and herds, figures of warriors armed with clubs, of hunters chasing antelopes, of men in canoes hunting hippopotamus. There were dance scenes, representations of libations, and so forth.

In a word, we were confronted with the greatest museum of prehistoric art in the whole world. There were pictures of extraordinary aesthetic quality (e.g. the lifesize women at Jebbaren and Sefar) such as would not discredit the finest schools of art in any age.

Two main art-styles stand out from the mass of paintings. One is symbolic in character. It is the more ancient and is apparently the work of Negro artists. The other is more recent. It is frankly naturalistic and in it influences from the Valley of the Nile are discernible. However, one very important thing about these paintings is that they are in no way related either to those of the Franco-Cantabrian area in Europe, on the one hand, or to the paintings of southern Africa on the other. Moreover, if at one stage Egyptian (and maybe also Mycenaean) influence can be observed, the most archaic of the Tassili pictures belong to a school unknown up to now and one that apparently was of local origin. The pictures of this latter phase afford us the most ancient data that we have concerning Negro art.

Again, although the paintings of the Franco-Cantabrian region have revealed to us something of the manners and customs of the palaeolithic cave-men, these pictures have not taught us much about the character or the origin of the artists, except that we do know that, at one time, France was inhabited by men who hunted bison, mammoth, rhinoceros and reindeer. However, if it be compared with our prehistoric European art, the Tassili art constitutes a mass of documentation which allows us to form a clear idea of the ancient populations of the Sahara, of the different types of peoples which swept over the desert in successive waves of herdsmen. We can also note the foreign influences which made themselves felt. Again, thanks to the Tassili pictures, we can follow the changes in the fauna and, thus, of the climate. We can trace the progress of that desiccation which was to culminate in the pitiless desert of today.

Here we have a discovery of extreme importance. At least eight millenia in the history of the world's greatest desert—and paradoxically in the history of man—have suddenly been made intelligible to us.

I

Saharan Perspectives

W<small>E HAVE</small>, quite recently, heard a good deal about the Sahara. We have been told much about its mineral riches and its oil. All of this makes us think of the desert, rightly or wrongly, as a new El Dorado.

Indeed, prospecting parties follow on, one after the other. Never have so many people been travelling in the desert as now. The most varied means of transport are used from the modest jeep (very useful for reconnaissance on almost any sort of terrain) to the helicopter employed by geologists looking for uranium deposits. And we must not forget the huge Bréguet two-deck trucks which bring to the drilling sites tons of food and cool drinks. It all contrasts very vividly with the conditions of primitive existence known to 'Saharans' only a few short years ago.

A charming lady sitting next to me in the plane from Algiers to Paris, when she learned that I had been conducting 'researches' in the Sahara, took me at once for an oil-man or a uranium prospector. I then told her something about what my own work was, but her first reaction indicates clearly enough the ideas people hold today about the great desert of Africa. It is true that the contrast between the aridity of the Sahara's soil and its suddenly revealed subsoil riches is enough to strike anyone's imagination, but we shall see that the most vast desert in the world still retains many of its secrets and that its present-day desolation is only

a passing phase of its long existence, once intimately bound up
with human life and rich in human history.

For more than twenty-five years past I have spent my time
travelling all over the Sahara. I have crossed the unending *regs*—the
real, rocky wastes—where you may march for a fortnight without
ever coming across trace of water. I have climbed all the Saharan
mountains, the Hoggar, the Tassili n'Ajjer, the Adrar of the Iforas
and the Ir. I have journeyed through the vast *ergs*—the sand-dune
areas—and especially in the Great Eastern Erg, a real sea of sand
with waves for ever ruffled by the winds. It is the most stupendous
accumulation of sand on this earth. I have followed the bed of
ancient Saharan rivers whose very complicated network is now but
a dry skeleton. I have also lived for long periods with the Tuareg
and the Mauretanians whose joys and sorrows I have shared on
those highways and byways of adventure where they served me as
guides.

I found this life enthralling. Everything was exciting, the
fauna, the flora and, of course, the unending problems of human
and physical geography, ancient history and the like, for the
Sahara is a whole which can be understood only in the light of
a mass of knowledge acquired in all sorts of fields, geological,
biological, climatological—and just human.

Most of my journeys were undertaken on camel-back and the
camel still remains by far the best means of transport if you want
to go everywhere and see everything in detail as a really serious
researcher must. Up to the time that I wrote this book I had done
50,000 miles in the Sahara (that is twice the distance round the
globe), 50,000 miles on camel-back. It is an archaic way of getting
about and it must be admitted that it involves a good deal of walking and leads to incidents some of which, in my case, might have
turned out very badly indeed. I have also driven by car through
several regions and I have, on many occasions, flown over the
desert. I think, then, that I may say I know the Sahara pretty well,

1. In the Sefar Massif

2. *On the Track from Sefar to Tamrit*

3. *The Expedition's Guides and Tuareg*

and although, on occasion, it has been very hard on me, then, again, it has behaved like a bounteous prince and has allowed me to raise some of the veils that shroud its mysterious past. Indeed, the whole problem for the Saharan explorer is this: to understand the desert of today in terms of what it was formerly.

Undoubtedly, what has always aroused my keenest interest and given me the greatest pleasure has been the human aspect of the desert, and especially its prehistory. Many and many a time I have discovered abundant evidence left behind them by ancient populations which lived in the valleys and mountains, hunted and fished and tilled the soil in different places and at different periods according to their various modes of life.

Right in the heart of one of the *ergs*—the Ténéré—I have come across the remains of fishers' encampments marked by formidable collections of fish bones (enough to fill several farm-carts), of hippopotamus and elephant bones with which were mingled the remains of hearth ash and stone implements.

Over three hundred miles farther south, on the fringes of the Sahara and the French Sudan, I discovered in more than ten camp-sites, fish bones, tortoise shells and those of molluscs, bones of hippopotamus, giraffe and antelope amid which lay human skeletons, whose position among the detritus showed clearly enough that the early Saharan populations did not practise what is called 'intentional burial'. Moreover, scattered about this prehistoric charnel-house was an abundant and magnificent stock of stone implements, many of which I collected . . . delicate arrow-heads in flint, gauges for fishing nets and also superb bone harpoons.

To the south of the Hoggar, at the foot of the In Guezzam cliffs, in a region which, at the present time, is one of the most pitiless and arid of all the Sahara, I made still another discovery of a similar sort; human skeletons and animal bones, while the

B

surrounding soil was covered with thousands of fragments of pottery.

I could cite many other examples since the prehistoric sites I have been able to identify in the Hoggar region amount to almost eighty.

From all this, then, we may conclude that, in former times, the Sahara was fairly thickly populated and that it contained a fauna similar to that still to be found in the savanna country beyond the desert's southern limits. If some of the ancient remains found date back in all probability several hundreds of thousands of years (as in the case of the vestiges of the fishers in the Admer *erg*), the most recent relics are possibly not more than four or five thousand years old[1]—that is to say that, archaeologically speaking, they belong to yesterday.

The aquatic character of the predominant fauna indicates surroundings which were damp and the existence of numerous rivers in full flood. Such rivers, taking their rise in great mountain masses such as the Hoggar, the Tassili and the Adrar of the Iforas, constituted a vast hydrographic system linked up with the Niger, with Lake Chad and with those great lakes whose shrunken remnants are to be seen in the *chotts* of the Tunisian south. It is still quite possible to plot out the courses of these streams. Indeed, I have flown in an aeroplane from the Hoggar and was able to follow the length of one of the fossil rivers clearly recognizable from its white furrow scoring the sands. By keeping to this course I reached, without any difficulty, the Niger near the town of Gao.

Prehistoric sites, heaps of rubbish thousands of years old, are not the only traces left by the ancient inhabitants of the Sahara.

[1] The Admer *erg* site is one of the two palaeolithic stations found *in situ* in the central Sahara and it is to the north of the Hoggar between that massif and the Tassili. The other site is that of the Tihodaine *erg*. (Author's note.)

There is also, on the rocks of the main mountain masses, and often in most deserted and desolate spots, evidence of their artistic ability in the shape of engravings and paintings, many of which are very fine.

I have copied hundreds of these ancient pictures into the pages of my diaries and they are most instructive for they belong to various periods and span, in time, the space of several millenia. These pictures confirm, to a great extent, what we can learn from the remains of ancient dwelling-sites and they afford us a mass of additional information regarding the types of cultures which have succeeded each other in the desert: cultures of hunters armed with clubs and boomerangs; cultures of herdsmen and archers; cultures of warriors whose arms were javelins and who introduced the domestic horse into Africa.

As can be seen from this evidence also, weapons have played a dominant part in the development of human societies. Arms are essential evidence, classical guides for the archaeologist. By the distribution of weapons we can estimate the importance of such and such a migration, we can trace the routes followed, and, in certain cases, we can trace the caravan tracks which, more than a thousand years before the beginning of our era, linked the Mediterranean seaboard with the banks of the Niger—as I shall point out later on.

This brief introduction will enable the reader to imagine what an extraordinary adventure it was to discover all these different data which explain and throw light upon each other, and the excitement that seized us as each new fact threw further light on the immense past of the desert, hitherto almost unsuspected. Had it not been said that the Sahara was the bed of an ancient sea and one of those cursed regions on our earth from which Man had always been excluded? Of course, there is not a word of truth in this fable. During the Pleistocene, or Quaternary, Period there never was any sea in the Sahara (and that means for the last million years at least), but the legend of the Saharan 'sea' has a tough life and seems to be as firmly anchored in popular belief as the Loch Ness monster, the lost Atlantis and many another story just as untrue. Indeed, the 'evidence' for a Saharan sea (during the period of Man's life on this earth) is quite illusory, for the oyster-shells which are to be found in great quantities in some regions of the desert date back to far-off ages in the Tertiary Period, that is to say geological epochs long before Man made his appearance on the globe.

The salt found in some Saharan depressions is the product of evaporation from the waters of lakes which had, first of all, washed over Primary and volcanic rocks rich in certain sulphates. The sands of the *ergs'* dunes owe their origin to erosion caused by intense water action (in very ancient times when the climate was wet) and the sands have been shifted and piled up by wind action in the most low-lying parts of the vast Saharan continental mass.

No, the Sahara has not been at any time, at least since Man existed, under the waters of the sea. The Sahara, however, has known, as have been many other portions of the earth, periods of great prosperity, and then disastrous morrows of harsh desiccation.

What, we may ask, was the reason for the desiccation? What caused this alternation of climate? This is the first question that comes to mind. But it must be admitted, straight away that the query admits of no brief and concise answer, for we are confronted with a complex problem, many of whose elements are still obscure and far from having been satisfactorily settled. The simplest explanation—though it is one which does not answer all the problems —is that there was, at a given period, a marked lack of balance between the water from rains and the very great evaporation induced by a remarkably high temperature. This meant disaster for the Sahara, and it can be foreseen what an unfortunate part would be played by the trade-winds which induced currents of cold air in the winter and of hot air in the summer, and so chased away the clouds and life-giving rains. A number of other factors should, however, be taken into account, such as the absence of mountain chains near the littoral which might have arrested clouds blowing up from the ocean, and also the existence of certain climatic factors related to zones of high and low pressure. But these, to tell the truth, remain rather enigmatic since thousands of years ago the Sahara had a far less arid climate than now, so that what is really difficult to explain is the relatively recent change in Saharan climate.

How many millenia have we to consider? I think that we shall know a little more about these matters when the data brought back by my last expedition have been examined and when the charcoal recovered from the newly discovered prehistoric sites has been subjected to radio-carbon tests.

What we know from the accounts left by ancient geographers, Greek and Roman, is that some five centuries before our era the Sahara was already in an advanced stage of desiccation. Herodotus, indeed, who lived in the fifth century B.C. (and who was the first to write of the lands lying to the interior of the continent and to the south of the Gulf of Syrtis), mentions regions of dunes, oases, inhabited areas and domes of salt. Strabo, 400 years later, noted that horses were still common in the Sahara, but he mentioned also that the nomads had to take many precautions on their wanderings and that they must sling water-skins under the bellies of their mounts, and this suggests that the precious liquid was becoming hard to find. The elder Pliny, writing a little later than Strabo, relates (A.D. 23–79) that elephant, giraffe and carnivorous beasts still existed in what he called 'Libya'—that is to say the whole of the *Maghreb* or the lands lying to the west of Egypt—but, on the other hand, when he describes the country of the Garamantes (which would be, apparently, what we now call the Tassili and the Fezzan) he mentions that the *wadis* no longer ran water except on occasion and that the water-holes were seasonal—in fact, that conditions were, as far as the hydrographic system was concerned, more or less as they are today. It is, however, true enough that at the beginning of our era the Sahara was more alive than it is now, the population was larger, the water-holes were nearer together, the plant life was less scanty, for horses could still subsist and this would be quite impossible today without all sorts of special precautions.[1]

However, the Sahara in the days of these ancient authors was already considered as a desert. It is, indeed, from their days that the famous legend dates of the Sahara being the bed of an ancient sea, for the sand of the dunes, the salt of the *chotts*, the oyster-shells on the Tertiary *hammadas*—rocky, pebble-strewn, low plateaux— had already made their impression on men's minds, on those of people who had, of course, only the very vaguest ideas about geology and the composition of soils.

The above is a short summary of our knowledge of the Sahara's past and it was in this setting that, for sixteen months, the members of the Tassili expedition lived out their unprecedented adventure.

Actually, the adventure had a number of episodes. The first idea of the expedition dates back to 1933 when Lieutenant Brenans (*see* p. 27) ventured into a deep canyon of the Tassili n'Ajjer during a police operation and found himself in a valley called Ighargharen lying to the south of the military post of Fort-Polignac. The Tassili n'Ajjer is a very large mountain mass situated to the north-

---

[1] Hence the substitution of the camel for the horse, the former seems to have been, a little before the beginning of our era, introduced from the Nile delta into which it had been imported from Arabia. (Author's note.)

east of the Hoggar and the canyon in question was called the Oued Djerat.

At the time I am speaking of the gorge had never been visited by any Europeans. Brenans, at the head of his detachment, was riding slowly along on his camel when he noticed, on the rocky walls of the *wadi's* cliffs, strange figures, the like of which he had never seen in the course of all his excursions. He dismounted and thought he must be dreaming. There before his eyes cut deep into the rock was a series of engravings of enormous animals, elephants walking along with their trunks raised, rhinoceros with ugly looking horns on their snouts, giraffes with necks stretched out as though to browse on the tips of the spiny bushes growing round about . . . in a word, an astounding spectacle in a deep corridor calcined by the sun and over which hung the heavy silence of a deserted land from which all human life had fled centuries before.

After a march of about six or seven miles, Brenans came up against a huge barrier of scree and debris that proved to be impassable, but he had, just the same, discovered one of the most magnificent and remarkable collections of prehistoric engravings in all the Sahara.

It is true that before Brenans' find many engravings had been recognized on rocks, especially in the Hoggar, in the south of the Algerian province of Oran and in the Fezzan, but nothing so fine or so extensive had been noted as what Brenans saw in the Oued Djerat. Side by side with beasts depicted in clear and elegant lines were human figures of very varied types. Some of them had animal heads. The find as a whole, indeed, was something quite novel. Furthermore, in little cells cut into the flanks of the rock-face (that must have served as shelters for mouflon hunters) Brenans had also noted very delicate paintings which were also something quite new.

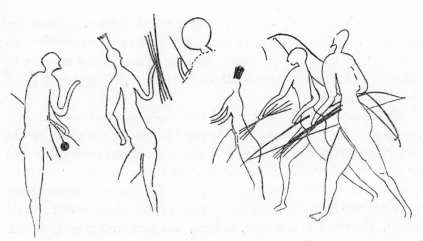

3a. Two Sketches of Frescoes from the Portfolio of Colonel Brenans

Of course, the experts in Paris and Algiers were informed of the discoveries and four months later I myself was on the spot at the same time as Professors Gautier, Reygasse and Perret, who stayed for several weeks on the Tassili. But I did not leave until a year and a half later.

A new page of Saharan history had opened for research.

2

Headed for the Tassili

COLONEL CARBILLET, who for ten years reigned, one may say, over the Sahara (and whose portrait Frison-Roche has painted as the *grand patron* in his novel *Montagne aux Ecritures*), greatly encouraged my wanderings in the desert and, as often as possible, let me take part in the reconnoitring parties he headed.

'All your researches into the past, all your studies of Tuareg life, your hunting for plants and little animals, what the hell do you think that means to us?' he would say in his grumpy manner. 'What we want here is engineers, geologists, what we need is roads, water, water most of all, that's all the Sahara wants.'

But such words were said half-jokingly, and as a matter of fact everything about the Great South interested him keenly. He was often rude, even churlish, but he was essentially good-natured, and endowed, moreover, with a sound common sense that he owed no doubt to his peasant origins. All told, he was eccentric enough, but he had a heart of gold.

'Look here, Lhote, get out once and for all from this damned Hoggar where you're stuck and bogged down. There can't be much about the place you don't know; come and see what's to be seen in the Tassili, no one ever goes there. You'll not regret it.'

Thus it was Carbillet who first revealed to me Brenans' discoveries and thus it was that a few months after this conversation I found myself on the Tassili. I was shivering in an icy wind, and I was down in the deep, dark gorge of the Imihrou. It had to be admitted that the Tassili was as wildly beautiful as the Hoggar and I fell under the spell of a country that is so strange, so lunar in its appearance. Rock-crusts calcined in a furnace and stripped, sandstone that nature had been pleased to carve into the most odd and fantastic shapes and forms. The Tassili is a world apart, one of the Sahara's precious jewels; perhaps, from some points of view, even more lovely than the much-vaunted Hoggar, more grandiose with its gigantic canyons and its deep-cut gorges filled with scree and rubble. In a week's hard marching a Tuareg guide and I covered the distance between the military posts of Fort-Polignac and Djanet situated respectively to the north and south of the Tassili mountain mass. This trip gave me a first and general impression of the Tassili's appearance.

It was at Djanet that I met Brenans, who showed me his collection of copies and drawings (only just completed) of the Oued Djerat pictures. He offered, indeed, to put them at my disposal, but I was obliged to leave almost at once in order to take part in the first reconnaissance by car of the Ténéré (one of the most arid regions of the desert—about seven hundred and seventy miles without any water-hole); it was only several months later that I was able to go to Djerat in company with the geographer Professor Perret (now president of the French Geographical Society), whom the celebrated historian Professor Gautier had asked me to pick up at Fort-Polignac and guide through the Tassili.

What we saw on that occasion astounded us, for although I had had many opportunities of examining engravings during my earlier wanderings, I had never seen anything so extraordinary, so original, so beautiful. Gautier, who had, some time before, visited the lower reaches of the *wadi*, had baptized the Djerat 'the Vézère of the Sahara'[1] and we found his expression in no way

[1] Near the banks of the Vézère river in the Dordogne department of France are some of the most famed prehistoric sites: Les Eyzies, La Mouthe, Le Moustier, Lascaux, etc.

exaggerated. Indeed, the engravings exist in their thousands on both sides of the *wadi*. We have to go as far afield as the Libyan Fezzan to find any comparable prehistoric documents.

Moreover, we were able to see more than our predecessors since we moved much farther up the canyon. At one moment our way was barred by an abandoned palm plantation, called Nafeg, whose shoots of wild trees were so matted and tangled with lianas that you would have thought yourself in the heart of the virgin forest. 'We'll never get through that,' said Perret; 'we'd better turn back.'

'No, we'll get through all right, you've just got to have a little patience.'

Slashing about me with a matchet, I hacked a way through the mass of vegetation, but the blade made little impression on the tough climbing plants and on the date-palms, so that the going was very tiring indeed. My arms and hands were all bloody, my clothing thorn-ripped and in tatters, but I still kept on cutting away, and yard by yard some sort of a path opened before us. When there was at last a passage we took our camels by the bridle and I made our whole company, whether they liked it or not, move in single file through a Red Indian trail. That evening we camped on the fine sand of the *wadi*'s upper reaches which, until then, had never been trodden by the foot of any European. Our evening feast was composed of fried fish caught with a bent pin tied to a string (and with bits of dates as bait) in a nearby pond. Our efforts had not been in vain, for we saw some very fine engravings as well as red-ochre paintings protected from the weather in shelters and niches.

This visit to the Oued Djerat was a decisive experience for me. The engravings and paintings had given me a glimpse of the great importance such unexpected artistic creations would have for archaeology. The beauty of the pictures, their aesthetic value, had aroused in me, also, an enthusiasm which was to increase with the passing of time. Next, I carried on my investigations in the region to the north of Djanet where Brenans had told me that he had seen rock-shelters with paintings. For months I wandered about all over the Tassili and saw so many pictures that my supply of drawing paper was soon exhausted. Brenans himself was an excellent draughtsman, but the copies we made were only poor, small-scale sketches which gave but an indifferent idea of what we had seen—above all, our drawings afforded no idea of the harmony of colouring, of the ochres employed by the prehistoric artists. From that time onwards I was haunted with a dream that one day I should go back and with a team of collaborators, mostly painters, I should be able to make life-size copies so coloured as to be absolutely faithful to the originals. Only in such circumstances could these masterpieces (which but a few of us could hope to see) be placed at the disposal of scientists, artists and the cultivated public generally, people for whom the Tassili was, to all intents and purposes, inaccessible.

I went on wandering about in the Tassili, and these wanderings cost me all my supply of camels. Indeed, the four beasts which constituted most of my capital and furnished me with the means of carrying on my prospecting died, one after the other, worn out by harrowing marches on the pebbles of a land where there is almost no pasture at all.

Years went by. Various occupations kept me in other parts of the Sahara. The war came and I was called up as a member of the Hoggar camel-corps goum,[1] though Brenans, who had been promoted captain on the spot, was lucky enough to be able to travel from time to time in the Tassili. It was not until 1954 that he and I met again in the Moroccan village to which he had retired after

[1] A goum (French spelling) is, in North Africa, an auxiliary military force composed of natives with French officers.

leaving the Army with the rank of Colonel. Together we discussed my scheme in which my old teacher, the Abbé Breuil, was also keenly interested. So, on my return from a mission in the south of the Oran department of Algeria (whither I had been sent to study once more the important collection of prehistoric engraving in that region) I set to work to get things started.

Brenans had agreed to look after the organization of the expedition while I was to deal with the scientific and technical side. Breuil promised to come to Africa and to spend several weeks with us. I collected a team which was to consist of four painters and a photographer. Montparnasse supplied the artists, one of whom had already been in the Sahara. I showed them the sketches I had made during my previous visits to the Tassili and explained the work to be done. They were all excited at the prospect of adventure and agreed without hesitation to take part in our expedition.

A few details about each member of the team will show how each one fitted into the absorbing venture we were to share.

1. Georges Le Poitevin, forty-three years old, former student at the Schools of Decorative Art and of the Fine Arts of Paris. Had been several times in North Africa and had been a resident student at the Villa Abd-el-Tif.[1] He had, indeed, even been as far as the Tassili itself, whence he had brought back a number of *gouache* paintings. Le Poitevin was quite a character. He was fond of the sea (he was of Norman origin) and loved the Sahara, perhaps because its winds and solitude reminded him of the ocean. Both in Montparnasse and in the Sahara everyone called him Jo.

2. Claude Guichard, twenty-three years old, a native of Grenoble. Former student at the *Beaux-Arts* schools in Grenoble and Paris. A most skilful fresco painter, he had already contributed to the decoration of several churches in the Alpine regions of

[1] The Abd-el-Tif Villa at Algiers is a resident school for artists more or less comparable with the Villa Medici French School at Rome.

France. He looked the regular, classical Bohemian with a goatee beard and long hair. To all appearances calm and placid, but really extremely sensitive, so that if he saw a fly killed he felt sick. He was to see this happen very, very often, and maybe his sixteen months in the Tassili rather toughened him. A hard worker and a great pipe-smoker.

3. Jacques Violet, twenty years old—in fact he celebrated his twentieth birthday in the Tassili—born in Paris, a former student of the School of Applied Art. Before he joined up with us he had been engaged at Vallauris in decorating pottery more or less in the style of Picasso. Distinguishing characteristic, over six foot three tall. He had grown very quickly and, anyway, was too young to have had a very complicated life.

4. Gianni Frassati, thirty-two years old, Italian. A former student at the Fine Arts School in Milan and had lived for some time in Paris. A talented portraitist and painter. Was one of the artists for whom Gina Lollobrigida posed and he made a small fortune from the sale of her portrait to one of her admirers. This, however, did not prevent the ungrateful fellow from preferring Sophia Loren as an actress. Frassati is built, as the French say, 'like a wardrobe', over six foot tall and weighing (at the start of the expedition) about 230 lb. He hoped to slim down a little. He was not disappointed. In Paris he shared not only a studio with Claude Guichard, but also a taste for macaroni.

5. Philippe Letellier, just under twenty years of age. Parisian. He was the photographer and cinematographer of the mission. He was trained in the school of Natkin and has made thousands of photographs of Parisian children. He was the real tough lad of the expedition, or at least he claimed to be.

To this list I would have added the name of my old friend Brenans, but a month before we set out he died in my house. He was carried off by a sudden heart attack. I felt his loss most deeply, for it put an end to a Saharan friendship of more than twenty years' standing.

Preparations demanded several months of work and it is, perhaps, difficult to imagine all the problems which have to be met and to be solved in connection with an expedition whose members must live and work and move about for months on end in a most inaccessible desert land.

First of all came the problems of individual equipment and these must be tackled with due regard to the extremely variable temperatures, which may exceed 122° F. in the shade in the summer and fall to below 14° F. in the winter. Then came what may be called the technical problems, for the work we were to do necessitated a considerable supply of suitable equipment—drawing-tables, folding ladders, various materials for drawing, a stock of paper (about eight hundred square yards of it), colours, photographic supplies, cameras and so forth. When they were set up our tables measured over fifteen feet long, and when I told the Abbé Breuil of this he raised his hands to heaven and exclaimed, 'How on earth do you think you're going to get all that stuff up on to the Tassili?'

Then we had to think of foodstuffs and the purchase of the thousand and one things necessary for a team that would have to be self-supporting, objects ranging from penicillin to can-openers, and not forgetting hair-clippers. The whole consignment, stacked up in one of the offices in the Museum of Man that served us as a store-room, weighed three tons and we had to transport these three tons for 2500 miles, and to transport them, if possible, without spending any money, for we had to count every penny of the credits that had been accorded us. I managed, however, to perform this feat, thanks to the kind offices of a transport company, of a shipowner friend and of General Quénard (Inspector-General of the Algerian Southern Territories), who has always shown

4. The Tafalelet Pass

himself to be the providential friend of scientific missions in the Sahara.

The Abbé Breuil, the greatest authority in the world on prehistoric art, was to have been with us for a few months, but he finally had to give up his plan in view of his great age and the many calls on his time.

Thus it was that I had to see the whole thing through, but the moral assistance (and as a consequence of that, the material aid) he gave us was very great, and I must admit that without him we should never have been able to overcome the obstacles that we found in our path. The Abbé Breuil did not spare himself in his efforts on our behalf. He was everywhere our most influential supporter. We might indeed say that he was with us all the time, since every mail brought a message from him and he was kept regularly informed of what we were doing.

Our expedition was put under the aegis of the Museum of Man in Paris and its director, Professor H. V. Vallois, and Dr. Léon Pales, one of the assistant directors, used all their influence to help us and watched the carrying out of our task with friendly interest.

At the request of all the members of its ethnographical section, the National Centre of Scientific Research gave us financial support. In Algiers, M. Jacques Soustelle, then Governor-General of Algeria and a former assistant director of the Museum of Man (and as such peculiarly qualified to judge of the importance and usefulness of the work we had undertaken), accorded us his patronage. The civil and military authorities in Algiers did all they could to smooth our path. We owe them a deep debt of gratitude.

At the end of January 1956 we all left Paris and a few days later I disembarked at Algiers. While our three tons of baggage was being hoisted on to an army truck, a DC3 from the Maison-Blanche air base was put at our disposal by M. Max Lejeune (then Under-Secretary of State for Defence) and took us all in one hop to Djanet.

C

5. *Camp-fire at Sefar*

Mlle Irène Montandon joined us at the last moment in Algiers. She holds a certificate for proficiency in Berber and M. Soustelle had just helped her to satisfy a wish to live among the Tuareg and study their language. Mlle Montandon was with our expedition for three months and during that time acted as secretary. As there was a great deal of correspondence she was kept quite busy.

Henceforth the beautiful oasis of Djanet, at the foot of the Tassili plateau, was to be our only point of contact with the civilized world. From Djanet set out each month the convoy that supplied us with foodstuffs.

By 20th February 1956 about thirty camels had been collected for us, at the *bordj*, or fort, by the orders of the chief of the post, Captain Rossi, a friend of twenty years' standing, whom I met first in the Tassili during my wanderings of 1934. Five cameleers, all Djanet men, a Tuareg guide and two boys made up our staff. We got ready to leave.

The members of the team, although rather impatient and disconcerted by the mass of baggage that had to be hoisted on to the camels' backs, did their best. The camels grunted, chewed the cud and filled the air with the odour of their fetid breath and their defecations. The cameleers arranged the loads, pulled on straps and cords and cursed one another, for, of course, the aim of every man was to put the least amount of baggage on his own camel. The really heavy stuff was for the next beast, naturally.

I had lived so long among these men that I knew all their tricks well enough, and I managed to make some order out of the chaos, but all the same it took us almost half a day to get everything ready and for the caravan to set off.

In order to get up to the Tassili plateau (whose cliffs form a background, from 1600 to 2300 ft. high behind Djanet) you have the choice of four passes; only one of them, however, was practicable

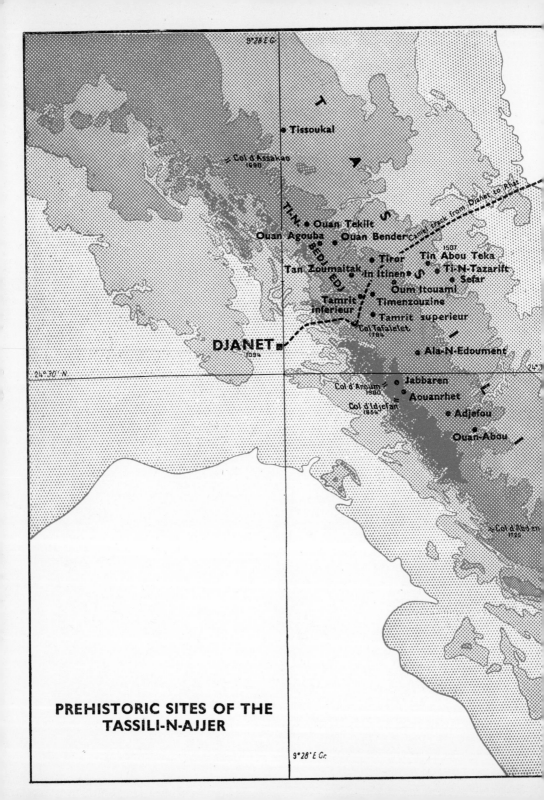

PREHISTORIC SITES OF THE
TASSILI-N-AJJER

for our expedition's baggage camels. Unfortunately the route we had to take was the farthest off and with the detour we had to make it took us a week to reach our first base camp. The early stages were short for the loads were not as yet properly adjusted, and it needed several days before everything was as it should be. My companions learned, without too much trouble, how to ride on camels and then, every evening, there was the encampment to be made. Little by little everyone found out how to put his sleeping-bag in place, how to blow up his pneumatic mattress and how to discover a spot where the baggage offered some protection from the glacial night wind, since, as long as we had not got to our operations centre, we did not set up our tents but slept in the open air.

Irène Montandon took charge of the commissariat arrangements; she gave the boys the orders for the meals. Everyone seemed to like the new, picturesque way of life. Morning and evening we gave some of our rations to the half a dozen chickens we carried—in cages. These birds were sacrificed as and when we needed them, though two of the chickens died of the cold. These the boys wanted to throw away but my companions intervened. After all, it was just frozen food, so we cooked the birds despite the boys' objections, and I must say that the stew did not seem any worse than any other we got.

The first three days' march, on easy ground, seemed to us later on, when we thought of it, just a pleasant walk. But soon we got to the foot of the Assakao Pass, up which we had to clamber and climb. The first day's journey in the mountains led us to a picturesque circle of hills, but it was too spacious, too open to all the winds of heaven, and, therefore, bitterly cold. Here we spent one of the most uncomfortable nights of all our experience. We pulled on thick jerseys and our padded *anoraks* and we were all smiling when our lady commissariat officer passed round a bottle of

brandy she produced from her sack. Then came boiling hot Vian-
dox and a supper prepared in a high wind and the dark. We felt a
little better when we slipped down into our sleeping-bags. The
camels, poor beasts, with streaming eyes and shivering in the cold,
were a good deal less comfortable than we were. In the morning,
we had to wait before setting off again, until the sun had warmed
up both animals and men. It was two in the afternoon when we
got to the foot of the main pass.

This was to be a great trial of endurance and as I knew the
place from of old I was sure that things would not pass off without
some misfortune. Each cameleer led his beast and the ascent began.
Amid huge masses of scree and rubble, the camels, in single file,
began their way up on a narrow path of crumbling soil. We could
see the animals, with their loads, seek a footing, and advance slowly,
held by the bridle by the men guiding them carefully through
the most difficult spots. Sometimes the camels had to be beaten to
force them over an obstacle while all the time arose cries and
shouts (the Tuareg of our party were good at that sort of thing);
in fact, one continuous roar issued from all throats. The beasts
strained and panted from their exertions. The path got steeper and
steeper. The masses of fallen rock ever larger. This was a real
torture for the camels. Several collapsed under their burdens and
rolled down into the ravine. Then all the cameleers got together,
pulled up the fallen animal and loaded it again, but no sooner had
this one got started up than another would fall a little farther on.
Soon we did not know where to turn. The men were needed
everywhere at once and the strain on them was almost too much
to bear.

Our guide, the Tuareg Sermi, who it must be admitted kept
strict discipline in his team, did not spare himself. He was
always there when there was something to be done. It is true
that he bawled aloud unceasingly, but he also worked like a slave.

He it was who got hold of the loads when they slipped off the camels and he it was who put the burdens on the beasts once more, and that often under the greatest difficulties and in places where there was hardly room for one man to pass.

We began to wonder whether we should ever get to the top. The camels were exhausted, and on the fallen rocks you could see plenty of smears of blood, for the beasts cut their feet and fetlocks on the stones' sharp edges. The camel that carried the big boxes with the drawing-tables crumpled under its burden, which had crashed against a rock. It was clear that the beast would never be able to rise again. Something radical had to be done, so I had the tables taken out of their cases. Since all this precious equipment could not be subjected to the risk of another fall and tumble among the rocks, I decided to have it carried on the men's backs. Each of the team got his share and then the calvary began, for the pass's summit was still far away while the stony path rose steeply under our feet. One after another the water-cans were emptied and the doses of dextrin disappeared rapidly. But the team-spirit was strong and everything passed off well enough. Other camels collapsed, more baggage had to be carried on men's backs, but each man had his heart in the job and we were quite sure that we should come through all right.

It was five o'clock in the afternoon when at last we got all our belongings to the top of the pass. Each one of us was dropping with fatigue. I marched serrefile, leading my own dromedary and pushing before me that of Le Poitevin that was an old beast almost at its last gasp. Then came a steep pull up of about ten yards. I had turned my head round to admire the fantastically beautiful panorama that lies before one at the head of the pass when the poor beast slipped on a stone and, being quite unable to right itself, slithered, with its legs in the air, down the slope and came to rest jammed against huge blocks of rock. I was able to side-step just in time so as not to be carried along in the camel's wake and be crushed beneath its heavy body. It needed all of us to get the beast on its feet again and to extricate it from its position. At last, after exhausting efforts and pulling at its legs and tail (which might have seemed absurd had not the animal's life been in danger), the wretched camel reached the summit of the pass. The creature was still trembling but was obviously relieved at not having left its bones to moulder at the canyon's bottom. Claude Guichard, the most sentimental member of the party, had tears in his eyes and turned away so as not to witness the sad spectacle. But he was destined to see many more of the same kind. The day was not finished. We had, once more, to right the baggage, reload the pack-saddles before we reached the nearest *wadi*, where we found sparse but healthy pasture. Then we pushed on in the darkness that had swiftly gathered. We stumbled against stones, and as the caravan had broken up into little groups, we went on without knowing much where we were until we made out the glimmer of the fire that Sermi—who had gone on ahead to spy out the land— had taken care to light so that it might serve as a beacon to rally the members of our party.

The wind was cruel, icy cold. Each one of us sought some shelter behind his baggage or took up his place round the fire. In silence, we munched on the dry dates the Tuareg offered us. That night none of us needed to be lulled to sleep.

3

The First Survey at Tan-Zoumiatak

'YOU have the *baraka*,' my old Tuareg guide, Jebrin-ag-Mohammed, said to me when he joined us a few weeks later at our Tamrit encampment.

He was right. 'Divine blessing' did seem to be with us.

For the past four years there had fallen practically no rain at all on the Tassili and the pastures were so burned up and desiccated that the Tuareg herds were reduced to half their numbers while the beasts which had survived were appallingly thin and scraggy. However, on the very day of our arrival at Djanet heavy clouds had swept up. They soon burst and emptied showers on the region lying to the north of the oasis so that the *wadi* not only began to run water but also to overflow its banks far and wide among the palm-trees.

As may be imagined, I was the first to rejoice at this, since without pasturage and without water in the rock-pools our stay in the Tassili would have been so disagreeable as to be almost intolerable. Thus it was with delight that we beheld the first flowers enliven, in little bright-coloured patches, the monotonous and sparse vegetation of the *wadis*. Our camels were as pleased as we were since they were the first to benefit by such rare good fortune. They did not stint themselves at our camp on the Assakao Pass.

My companions were, however, still hidden in their sleeping-bags and were obviously dubious about leaving them, for something had happened that is very seldom seen in the Sahara. A heavy dew had covered our bags and blankets and the sharp morning chill had frozen this dampness into a coating of ice.

It was quite a business to round up the camels which had scattered about in the neighbouring *wadis*. Thus our convoy did not get going again until about eleven o'clock in the morning. Anyway, during the slow marches where the pace was all the time made still more lingering by the fall of some piece of baggage, we decided to forgo a midday meal so as not to add to the delay. During a brief halt we just pecked at some sardines and biscuits washed down with green tea.

Now the landscape became monotonous. We were pushing across a bare plateau raked unceasingly by an icy wind and we had to keep on our *anoraks*. The camel which had had the accident, and was about at the end of its tether, advanced painfully far behind the main body of the caravan. The creature was pulled along by Jo—who obviously could no longer ride it—while he encouraged the beast's efforts by his strange cries. However, with this one exception, things went off fairly well. The first change in the relief of the ground appeared as rocky barriers. Then, soon, my companions burst into exclamations of admiration. We were, indeed, trudging through a veritable forest of sandstone columns. Gigantic pillars closed us in on every side. A fantastic, an indescribable, scene which our European eyes could hardly take in.

After all, just what is the Tassili? Its name in the Tuareg language means 'plateau of the rivers'. Sure enough, there is a plateau, but as for the rivers, well, that is altogether another matter. Today, anyway, you would look in vain for anything else but dried-up valleys. The structure of this mountain mass, that measures some five hundred miles long and varies in width from about thirty to

6. Sefar. Swabbing Down a Rock-face

7. I-n-Tifnar: Taking a Tracing

9. Sefar: Colouring of a Copy in the Headless Man Rock-Shelter

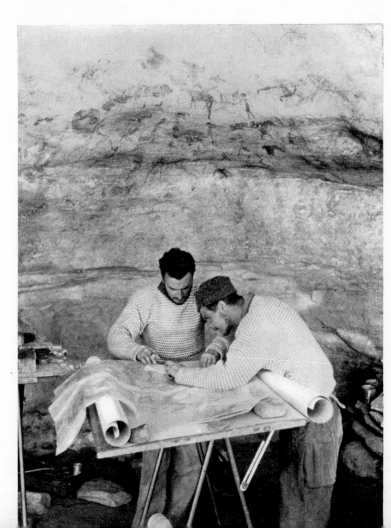

8. Sefar: Transfer of Tracing onto Drawing Paper

10. *Painted Rock-Shelter at Aouanrhet*

11. *The Great Shelter at Jabbaren*

forty miles, differs much from one area to another. The southern edge drops steeply to the Hoggar peneplain from which it rises, as I have said, in a wall that is from 1600 to 2300 feet high. The huge mass of friable sandstone of which the Tassili is formed has a north-south direction and therefore most of its valleys also run the same way. Many canyons, in the past, have been churned out by water-action and these are the deeper in that they are the farther from the heights. But water-action was not confined to scooping out gorges. The whole mountain mass was attacked and run-off waters hacked up the massif, cut it about in the strangest fashion, eroded it, scored it, pierced it and, in places, worked the huge block of stone into lace-like filigree.

Water-action, in a land where it hardly ever rains? Yes, water-action, but, of course, in the far distant past, for these sandstone masses have been in place for millions of years and have been exposed to the attack of the elements for countless epochs of time. The spectacular erosion does not, indeed, date from yesterday.

From this time onwards we were to be surrounded by fantastic scenery as we pushed forward. The lumbering convoy passed by tall columns that reminded us of the ruins of some medieval city with decapitated keeps, church spires, cathedral portals . . . with strange 'signs' like allegorical animals . . . a host of architectural elements each one more curious than the last.

After three days' march, we reached at last the amphitheatre of Ti-n-Bedjedj, after we had watered our beasts and renewed our own supply of water in a rock pool of the Oued Iddo, a legacy of the providential *baraka* rains.

This natural amphitheatre of Ti-n-Bedjedj measures about a thousand yards across and is surrounded by tall cliffs most of which are eroded at their bases. The natural cavities thus formed made very welcome shelters and there we took up our quarters. By this time, too, we had got to the area of the prehistoric paintings and even a rapid survey enabled us to discover hundreds of them. The general configuration of the terrain and the numerous recesses reminded us of a public square surrounded with houses. It was easy enough to realize why the populations of long ago made use of such a convenient arrangement.

What did we see on the walls of the shelters that surrounded us? Human figures of various sorts—some with European-type profiles, others with rounded and schematized heads and still more whose only head was a short stick—and animals (they occupy a prominent place in this prehistoric picture-gallery), giraffes, cattle, horses harnessed to war-chariots, other steeds mounted by riders armed with javelins, mouflon pursued by dogs, and so forth. Undoubtedly a number of different human groups must have lived in this area, when the climate was favourable, and each one of them had inscribed its story in its own manner, a manner that was dictated by the main preoccupations of the group. For some groups it was hunting, for others stock-raising, for others again war . . . what a contrast with the desert scenery that surrounded us!

Now for the first time since we had left Djanet we met with Tuareg encampments. When we arrived we noticed several flocks of goats led by little girls on their way back from the pastures. As night fell and we huddled round a fire while our boys prepared a meal, on the other side of the amphitheatre several caverns lit up and human shadows were thrown against the walls. For some minutes we really had the impression of living in prehistory and of being the contemporaries of the artists whose works we had been studying. A moving and weird illusion.

The next day I paid a visit to our neighbours. They were three families living in the rock-shelters and consisting only of women and children. The men were far away, most of them with caravans. The Tuareg, generally speaking, spend their nights under skin tents, but these Tassili Tuareg were very poor and wretched. They lived troglodytes' lives and sheltered from cold and wind behind the little stone walls they built. The flocks of goats are lodged in the same way as their masters.

Furniture consisted only of a few wooden utensils, an old iron cauldron, a blue enamel tea-pot, a few skin sacks of dry dates and millet, but the sacks did not look very full.

The women, after they had chased away the barking dogs, received me politely and offered me the milk of hospitality in a dirty bowl where I could make out not only grains of sand but also goats' hairs. But the ice was broken and a few minutes later the women and children invaded our camp and begged persistently for tea, sugar and flour.

Irène Montandon excited their special curiosity. She was literally mobbed. While one of the women felt the weight of Irène's blonde tresses, another enviously fingered at her scarf, while a third tried first to get her watch away from her and then seized hold of the bodice of her dress. One mischievous little thing went so far as to dive into Irène's pockets whence she drew forth string. a pencil (which she tried at once to steal), paper, and, luckily enough, dextrose.

Irène distributed a handful of dextrose tablets and amused herself by letting all the little party jabber away to their heart's content.

Three days' march and then we got to Tan-Zoumiatak, which was to be our first base camp. Except for the painful ascent of the Assakao Pass the caravan had moved forward without mishap. It is true that a few camels stumbled and fell, but there was no serious accident. We found that some of us had frozen fingers in the mornings and also that the more delicate skins got sunburned (Irène had a most beautiful red nose), but that sort of thing was easy enough to put up with.

Then our cameleers rounded up their beasts and when the men had been paid their wages and the hire of the camels they set off for Djanet and the pastures of the *erg*. I kept four camels, two dromedaries for reconnaissance work and for the mail and two pack-camels for transport.

We set up our tents for the first time and organized our camp for a long stay since here it was that our work really started.

At Tan-Zoumiatak there is a large rock-shelter with paintings which were already known, although the photographs which had been taken of them gave only a poor idea of the aesthetic quality of the pictures. When we entered this place (for it is rather a cavern than a shelter) we stood astounded at what we saw. Great human figures in yellow ochre, body and hair dotted with white, large mouflon in white and purplish-blue ochre, white animals with yellow ochre outlines—and of forms so curious and fanciful that they are practically unidentifiable—various human figures and a great many small animals. The whole was in an excellent state of preservation and we did not tire of admiring the curious shapes and the quality of the colouring. Without any doubt this was a miniature—and Saharan—Lascaux.

After a rather careful examination of the different figures I came to the conclusion that there were at least six different phases of pictures—phases which were revealed by superpositions and over-painting. These added very considerably to the interest of the whole assemblage and we decided to copy all the pictures just as they were. So, for a start, the artists were to have plenty of work. Without delay we brought up the tables, ladders and painting materials.

The boys, meanwhile, got settled in at the camp. Irène Montandon devised our menus—oh, of course, they did not offer much variety—and made a detailed inventory of the rations. The drudgery began. Fetching water and wood and baking bread. The water came from the pools and it contained all sorts of little

creatures swimming about in it—larvae of coleoptera, tiny crusta-
cea like very small shrimps . . . and then sand, grass with bits of
camel and goat dung. Galigala, one of the boys, who had a practical
turn of mind, filtered this rather impure liquid through the
chéchia[1] which he wore instead of a turban, a head-dress with
which, on occasion, he blew his nose, wiped his feet and the
crockery. Since he was so obviously well-intentioned and full of
good-will we had not the heart to protest. Anyway, in the Sahara
you cannot be too squeamish.

The work done on copying the Tan-Zoumiatak fresco (an
incomparable masterpiece worthy of a great museum) allowed our
team of painters to settle, once and for all, the technique of their
job. In view, too, of the exceptionally large surface covered by the
paintings—some thirty square yards—the very delicate task held
lessons for us all. The proceeding adopted was relatively simple.
First of all a tracing was made directly on the rock-face. Then this
tracing had to be corrected since the irregularities of the walls
caused distortion which had to be rectified. Then the background
tints were put in so as to reproduce the general setting of the
pictures, a setting that is peculiar to prehistoric paintings. Finally
the tracing had to be transferred on to paper and the figures
coloured in the presence of the originals. In this way nothing
was left to the personal whim of the copyist. This method, I think,
is the best and most reliable for rendering rupestral pictures as
faithfully as possible. In view of the size of the copy, we worked,
of course, on successive strips which afterwards were joined
together in the 'studio'. The difficulties we encountered were,
however, many, since the rock-face presents many bosses and
hollows. In fact the work takes a long time and demands not

---

[1] *Chéchia* is the usual French spelling of the Arabic word that designates the soft and
pliable 'fez' widely worn by North African Moslems—with, or without, an accompanying
turban.

only all the artist's skill but also his most careful attention. The reproduction of this Tan-Zoumiatak fresco took nearly a fortnight and the combined efforts of all our team. However, the result was excellent and from then on I was convinced that we were going to turn out altogether exceptional work; in fact, the sort of thing I had dreamt of for so long.

Now that we had really settled down to the job, I was the man-of-all-work. I organized, directed and checked the team's results. I also reconnoitred the surrounding region, looked for other painted sites and for such archaeological evidence as might enlighten us concerning the character and origin of the creators of the frescoes. As soon as I was no longer wanted in camp I set off with Sermi, our Tuareg guide, and explored the neighbourhood. Four hours by camel from Tan-Zoumiatak I penetrated, one day, into the Tin Abou Teka massif in which several prehistoric paintings had already been reported. The site is a little rocky citadel that dominates, from a height of some three hundred feet, the gorge below. This citadel is cut through with a number of narrow alleys in which, however, it is quite easy to move about. You get the impression of wandering in a dead and deserted city, though I did come across four Tuareg families living amid the winding passages in improvised dwellings protected by low walls.

What I saw on the alleys' walls left me thunderstruck. There were life-size figures painted in red ochre, archers with muscular arms and legs, enormous 'cats', many scenes with cattle, war-chariots and so forth. Up to this time I had never seen figures of this sort in the Tassili and the mass of paintings that I managed to view that day quite put into the shade all those I had seen up to then. I was full of enthusiasm when I got back to camp and told of my discoveries, which included three other fine rock-shelters I saw on my way back. All the same, we decided to put off copying these until later, since our programme called, first of all, for the reproduction of those pictures I had noted formerly at Tamrit, which is about an hour's march from Tan-Zoumiatak.

Guichard and I went off to settle in at Tamrit and lay the groundwork. We lived in a small grotto, did our own cooking and took tracings all day long from morning to evening. Sermi brought us food supplies regularly and Irène, who knew a short way round, did not hesitate to set out alone to come and visit us.

One morning a Tuareg in rags arrived at our camp and came towards me to shake hands. After a moment's hesitation I recognized in him my old guide Jebrin who had been with me in the Tassili twenty years before. True to tradition, we drank the tea of friendship and then I decided to sign him on as a member of the expedition.

Meanwhile the work at Tan-Zoumiatak was nearing its end. Every day Sermi brought up baggage on camel-back. Philippe Letellier was the first to join us, then came the tents and the rest of the team. After that, for the first time, we sent a courier to Djanet so as to give news of us to friends in Algiers and Paris.

Nowadays most of the expeditions in the Sahara have radio equipment, but I had decided that this was useless for us; the gear is cumbersome and a good deal of time must be spent on maintaining communications. After all, what did it matter to us what happened in Europe or the rest of the world? We might be out of touch in the ordinary sense, but we were in close and stimulating contact from morning to night with the prehistoric men of the Tassili.

4

The Cypresses of Tamrit

W E HAD, indeed, a sense of actually being in daily con-
ference with the prehistoric artists of the Tassili.

At Tamrit the surroundings are superb and differ a
good deal from those in other parts of the plateau. We took up our
quarters in rock-shelters or hollows overlooking the deep *wadi*
blocked here and there with masses of rock that bar the way to
camels. There was a pool only ten yards from our camp and this
afforded us, without any tiresome trudging about, the water needful
both for cooking and washing. An exceptional feature of Tamrit is
the presence of several magnificent cypresses whose trunks are more
than twenty feet in circumference and whose green foliage stands
out strikingly against the dull, burnt-brick colour of the surrounding rocks. The trees are scattered along the bed of the *wadi*.

Our Tuareg camped in a circle of rock near the fires. About
five hundred yards away we were surprised to find the most impressive waterfall in the Tassili; it is nearly eighteen hundred feet
high, and at its foot lay the silvery surfaces of several little lakes.
This particularly picturesque scene gave us some idea of what life
here must have been like in prehistoric times when the painters
decorated the rock-walls with scenes of hunting or of cattle on the
move.

Often enough, when night fell and the day's work was done,
we would come out of the grottoes and shelters, which all the
time afforded us new pictures, new images, and sit by the camp-

12. *Tamrit: Fresco of the Hunters (detail): Bovidian Period*

13. *Upper Tamrit: The 'Egyptian' Boat: Bovidian Period*

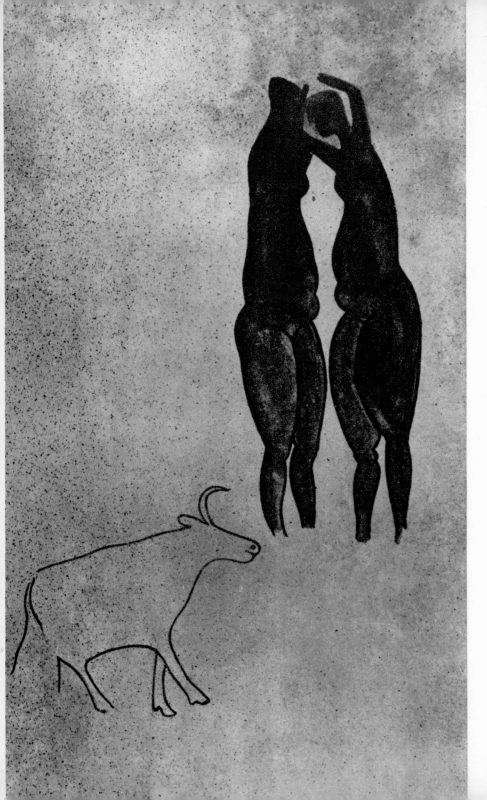

14. *Tamrit:
The Two
Venuses:
Bovidian Per*

15. *Upper
Tamrit: Th
Sable
Antelopes:
Bovidian Per*

fire. There we would conjure up, in our imagination, the grassy vales, the forest glades, the pools and all the beasts of what must have been an earthly paradise. We would picture to ourselves the placid elephants that flapped their huge ears while gathering round the pools, the timid rhinoceroses that followed the narrow paths to their lairs, the giraffes stretching their heads up into the trees, the antelopes and gazelles bounding about from one valley to another and grazing as they went or seeking out shade for rest. We would also imagine the men who lived near the rock-shelters, how they would get ready their arms for the chase, how they would make clothes out of skins, how their women would busy themselves with cooking and then go to wash their pots and pans or to bathe in the neighbouring ponds. We would think of the herdsmen guarding their flocks at pasture, leading their cattle to the water-holes, bringing them back at nightfall to the camp and putting them safely behind fences of wood and branches where they would be safe from the attacks of prowling wild beasts.

Carnivores, indeed, must have swarmed in these rocky laby-rinths with impregnable hiding-places and yet quite near creatures that offered an easy prey. Lions and panthers must have been terrible visitants, lords of the countryside and a terror to men. On these occasions I could not help thinking of the scenery and the conditions of life I had known, in earlier days, on the Adamaoua mountains of the northern Cameroons where there still exists a like fauna, enormous herds of cattle and Peul herdsmen.

The cypresses that stood out before us present one of the most strange curiosities in all the Sahara. In former times there were such trees in the Hoggar, where an old cypress trunk was found not so long since. At our halt in Ti-n-Bedjedj Sermi had thrown on the fire a log that soon spread a balsamic scent around us. The wood was a piece of *tarout*, a word used by botanists to designate familiarly a tree whose Latin name is *Cupressus dupreziana*. I had

D

16. Jebrin, the Expedition's Guide

never noticed any such trees in the region, but Sermi explained that there were, in the mountains nearby, many of these trees which had been long dead—had been dead, as he expressed it, years before he had been born. In a country where wood is so scarce, and therefore much sought after, it seems incredible that these ancient tree-trunks should have survived so long. But the reason for their survival is simple enough. The Tuareg possess no implement, no axe that is strong enough to cut or split the great trunks, for *tarout* is so hard and so close-grained that its wood does not perish nor is it attacked by insects. During our expedition I paid great attention to these trees, for they too are prehistoric and are the silent witnesses to much damper conditions in the past. Counts which have been made indicate that there are not more than about a hundred of these cypresses still existing, though they must, in times long past, have been common enough on the Tassili's crests.

During one of my earlier expeditions, Professor Maire, of Algiers University, had asked me to get him *tarout* seeds. After several attempts I was successful in obtaining some and today you may see in the Botanical Garden of Algiers University two fine *tarouts* some seventeen or eighteen feet high. Experiments undertaken at Montpellier have also given good results, so the *tarout* has been saved from extinction, for although the Tuareg cannot cut up the stout trunks they mutilate savagely the small branches, and this outrage generally results in the death of the trees.

So it is plain enough that the mountain masses of the Hoggar and the Tassili formerly enjoyed a Mediterranean climate. We must not, then, be astonished if the Tassili highlands were once inhabited by Man.

As we proceeded with our work we discovered a splendid fresco of cattle, painted in red ochre and white, representing sixty-five beasts moving as a herd and accompanied by their herdsmen. With the aid of Claude Guichard I began to copy this painting. The job was a most exhausting one, for the wind blew unceasingly. It whipped up our tracing-paper and forced us to begin all over again, time after time. We were so absorbed in our task that we hardly noticed it had begun to rain and that puddles were forming in the valley.

Frassati, Le Poitevin and Violet were painting away in a profound shelter by the Oued Tamrit. Gianni was hard at work reproducing a magnificent scene in which hunters with painted bodies and armed with bows were chasing herds of antelope that, curiously enough, were represented only by their heads. Two others of our team were copying a fresco in which were shown human figures with round heads as well as representations of mouflon.

The great cattle fresco gave us unending trouble. It was nearly forty feet long and thus obliged us to copy it on parallel strips of paper which were extremely difficult to join up, since many of the beasts were, so to speak, cut in two. Still, everything would have gone well enough if it had not been for the accursed wind that made everything more complicated. We had to use big stones to hold down the paper and we had to steady the water-pots in the same manner. The damned wind not only ripped up the tracing-paper but also the drawing-sheets, and so, sometimes, destroyed in a few seconds the work of several days. This happened to a copy of a fresco of giraffes just finished off by Violet.

Often the paintings were so high up, ten feet or so from the ground, that we had to use ladders. At other times the pictures were in very low-roofed shelters so that we had to crouch uncomfortably on all fours. In every case when we had performed all the necessary acrobatics we were bruised and stiff. However, the most difficult and the most delicate task was that of reading the paintings aright, since generally they were very faded and, in cases, almost destroyed. There was only one thing to be done. The rock-faces must be washed so as to remove the clayey dust which had accumulated on them during the course of millenia. Then we had to brighten the colours by dabbing them with vegetable sponges soaked in water. By the naked eye alone, or with the use of magnifying-glasses, we managed to trace every inch of the original painting, but therefore we had often to spend many days in front of one single picture, especially as we were at the mercy of very varying lighting conditions. Sometimes the glare was dazzling, at other times it was so dark that it was even more difficult to see.

It was by repeated washing of the walls, that we were able to make our most remarkable discoveries. Some paintings, indeed, under their coating of dust were quite invisible to the naked eye.

Ever since we had left Djanet we had lived, mostly, on the supplies we had brought with us, but now we were beginning to run short of flour and, most of all, of fresh meat, since the Tuareg would not willingly part with even their oldest goats. Therefore Gianni, Sermi and the boy Galigala were sent off to Djanet to bring back everything eatable they could lay hands on. They set off with our four camels and took the track by the Tafalelet Pass—even more difficult than that of Assakao. I had confidence in Gianni. He was fond of good food and he was a resourceful fellow. During the three days he stopped at Djanet he levied toll on all the messes, he got into the good graces of the shopkeepers; in fact, he was so untiring in his efforts that our four camels came back loaded up with nearly nine hundred pounds of provisions, over two hundred of which were flour. There were also forty cans of preserved meat. However, if the way down was not so bad, the way up was dreadful because of the steep gradient and the loose stones and pebbles with which the track was strewn. At the third pass the beasts could not make any further headway and refused to budge. Despite all their cries and efforts Sermi and Galigala could not get the animals more than twenty yards forward. Then, to make matters worse, one of the camels fell down, and no sooner had it been got on its feet and reladen than it fell once more. There was no use trying again and the men, too, were quite exhausted. Nevertheless, they decided to take the loads off the camels and to carry the baggage on their own backs. There was no question of making a halt on so narrow a track. So the appalling task had to be performed. After that, the men had to go back and lead up the camels, which, now that they were no longer burdened, proved a little more tractable. Night closed in almost suddenly as the little company reached the top of the pass, but alas, there was no wood for a fire or any food for the beasts. So the party staggered on until they were so harassed and confounded by the ever-deepening darkness that they had to halt. Then each man slumped down on a heap of stones and with an empty belly dropped off into fitful slumber.

This damnable torture was to be inflicted on us quite twenty times during the expedition and each time the journey up the passes was a real nightmare. The Tafalelet Pass alone put eight camels out of commission. The Adjefan Pass was hardly any better and on one trip we lost three camels there. Two experiments made with asses through the Aroum Pass were hardly any more satisfactory, since the donkeys we had hired at Djanet were not used to rocky and stony paths, so that we had, once again, to carry up the stores on men's backs. Then came a time when Jebrin could not find any more camels since the Tuareg would not let any out on hire because of the numerous accidents. Thus it happened that for two whole months we could not get regular supplies. Rations had to be cut down to a minimum.

In fact, our Tassili expedition had to suffer all along from difficulties due to the very nature of the country. Not only did we have to help out the pack-animals when these were in no fit state to negotiate the passes, but also, when we got to our destination, we had, almost daily, to carry our drawing-tables, for hundreds of yards, or even, as at Tamrit, for over a mile.

Well, one could say that except for this sort of thing our troglodytes' life went on what might be called 'normally'. We suffered from the cold, we were often too hot, not seldom we went hungry, we worked very hard and plenty of times we felt that we should drop down with fatigue, but still, all that was in the day's work. Luckily, none of us died (though a death on an expedition is often good publicity), which was as well both for the sake of the possible victims and also for the leader of the expedition! Still, all this does not mean that our existence was carefree by any means.

Claude Guichard, for instance, developed a strange knack for finding a scorpion under his sleeping-bag nearly every morning, I do not know just what it was in him that attracted these repulsive creatures, but he brought me specimens of all shapes and sizes, black, white and brown—in fact a whole collection that would have delighted an entomologist. Maybe Guichard diffused some special 'fluid', some peculiar scent? Malicious members of our team declared that it was his beard that allured the scorpions . . . at first I thought that he was handing out prize-money to the Tuaregs for catching the creatures to excite and astonish us. But Claude is a serious-minded boy and quite incapable of such tricks. Luckily, it was never necessary to use the anti-scorpion venom serum we had in our kit, especially as the Djanet doctor had assured me that the serum made one much more ill than the bite itself.

We saw a great many vipers, for they swarm in the Tassili. These rocky solitudes are their true home and they take up their quarters in a *wadi* or a grotto. They hide under the hot sand during the day and glide about after nightfall. Their prey consists of lizards, geckos or birds that do not pay much attention to the little heap of sand that marks the viper's resting-place. The only enemy the vipers have to fear is Man. The Tuareg kill them without mercy. These reptiles, indeed, have a very bad reputation, and there is hardly a book on the Sahara which does not describe the horned viper as a hideous beast, terrifying and possessing 'death-dealing breath'. Was not the Hydra of the ancients a viper? All absolute rubbish. The viper is the meekest and gentlest animal on earth if you do not touch it. I might say, indeed, that the viper is among the most cowardly of creatures. Here is an example of what I mean. At our Timenzouzine camp a splendid specimen of a viper nearly three feet long lived for several days about six feet from my sleeping-bag. We must all have walked within a foot of the snake and none of us noticed it. Never did the poor 'Hydra' budge. It showed itself, indeed, remarkably retiring, but I finally did see it one morning. It was nicely curled up near a big stone, its body hidden in the sand and only a little tip of its head projecting. I took it upon me to break up this peaceful coexistence for I thought that after all there might be some unfortunate accident. Jebrin was delighted. He had loathed all vipers since, years before, one of them had bitten his foot and one of his legs had remained slightly paralysed. However, this misfortune gave him (strictly between ourselves) an admirable excuse for not observing the fast of Ramadan.

5

A Herdsmen's Culture

JEBRIN, in fact, was a strange man, intelligent and very much of a character. He was about sixty-five years of age (he was not very sure of the year of his birth), and had the reputation of being the greatest lady-killer in all the Tassili. He had two wives, a young one and an old one, and at least ten children. Furthermore, he had red hair—that is very rare among the Tuareg —and because of this was suspected by his fellow-tribesmen of being the son of a *jinn*.[1] Generally speaking, the Tuareg have raven-black hair, so red hair can be explained only as the result of diabolical intervention. Jebrin's mother must have been the sport of one of those thousands of malign spirits which, in the Tuareg's ingenuous imagination, people their mountains.

However, such a reputation did not prevent Jebrin from being gay and full of go, despite his rheumatism. I was never bored in his company. He was the teller of innumerable stories. Moreover, he knew my habits and customs so that when we went off together he forestalled my every need without my ever having to give him any orders.

In 1934 and 1935 we had travelled together over the Tamrit region and he had then been amused at my inspecting the walls of the rock-shelters and even the smallest grottoes. He watched with a rather detached air my scrambles among the rocks. For him

[1] A *jinn* is Arabic for a spirit, generally an evil one; a demon.

such conduct was just a sign of the odd manias which, in the eyes of the Tuareg, so often afflict the French. The Tuareg consider that a botanist who collects plants or a biologist who dips his net into pools (to collect the larvae of *Diptera*) are people who are at a loss for something to do in life. According to the Tassili nomads' code the only respectable occupations for a man are drinking, eating, sleeping and indulging in the pleasures of love whenever an opportunity offers.

Jebrin was all the less interested in my prospecting, since when I would call him to come and see one of my discoveries he could understand nothing at all about the picture I showed him on the wall. Horses harnessed to a war-chariot? What image could that arouse in his mind? He had never, in all his life, seen many animals but camels, asses and goats. The past? What past? For him the past was nothing but a jumble of traditions, struggles between rival tribes that date back, at the most, a few generations. The distant past, that is something which does not enter into the Tuareg's thoughts. The pangs of hunger in their bellies give them enough worry without their thinking about the past.

Jebrin just understood that when he saw a picture of horns that the body which bore them must be that of an ox or an antelope, animals fairly familiar to him since he had seen them on his trips to the French Sudan. One day, when I had just discovered the outline of an elephant, I pointed it out to him.

'There's the head, Jebrin, here's the trunk and there are the tusks. Don't you see them?'

But Jebrin saw nothing at all and understood nothing at all, although the picture was plain enough, for if he had heard about the existence of the giant pachyderms (elephants indeed have a place in Tuareg folklore) he had no idea at all of their shape.

However, since that time, Jebrin had become infected with the archaeological virus and no longer disdained hunting for *surat—*

an Arabic word that means 'images' and was applied by him to rupestral paintings. He kept a sharp look-out and he got into the habit of inspecting the rock-shelter walls he came across during his peregrinations.

All the same, I knew well enough that I had not made a disciple out of him and that he had no ambition to belong to the French Prehistorical Society or to publish his discoveries—for he remained quite impervious to their significance. Maybe, however, he had another aim, that of showing his finds one day to tourists who might venture into his domain. There might be money in that.

Still, in one sense I had made a disciple, for Jebrin now became my most useful collaborator. He came with me and helped me each time that I went off on a prospecting expedition. While we were on the track he would not stay still a minute, but was for ever off to rummage about in the *wadis*, visit the neighbouring rock-shelters . . . then he would hurry back to me. 'There's something here, there's something there.'

His stories could not always be taken at their face value, but he did, so to speak, clear the decks, and that was an appreciable service. There is no doubt at all that, thanks to him, we made our discoveries much quicker; indeed so quickly did he find new sites that even the artists were hard put to keep up with him.

We made two fine discoveries, one very soon after the other. The first was that of the rock-shelters in the Oued Timenzouzine (to the north of Tamrit) and the second was that of the shelters in the upper reaches of the Oued Tamrit itself.

At Timenzouzine the *wadi* runs between two walls of cliff whose bases are deeply eroded so that they form a continuous row of shelters that runs for about a hundred and seventy yards on either side of the river-bed. When I first saw this site I could hardly contain myself for excitement since there were to be seen hundreds and hundreds of paintings . . . fish several yards long, giraffes, elephants, delightful-looking archers dashing forwards at the run, and then oxen, more and more oxen, in an interminable procession.

In the neighbouring corridors we found still other paintings. There were also some in the rock hollows situated half-way up the cliff-face. These we had to reach by a series of acrobatic feats. There were, indeed, pictures everywhere. Never anywhere in any area of prehistoric art have there been reported so many figures on one and the same rock-wall. There are, maybe, a thousand figures belonging to a dozen different art-styles. One of the most curious pictures at which I gazed for long represented a sorcerer with mouflon's feet.

A few days after this, while I was looking for a grotto I had seen before and in which were pictures of elephants, Jebrin called to me to say he had just seen something 'very pretty'.

I ran to join him. The something 'very pretty' was an immense tapestry, a magnificent assemblage of antelopes treated in what might be called an heraldic style (and recalling certain Renaissance paintings). It is a frieze that will be famous one day, for it is a masterpiece of Tassili art. It is situated in the corner of a tiny shelter, all of whose walls from top to bottom are covered with paintings.

The Tassili peoples had plenty of decorative taste and quite evidently they knew how to paint. But just why did they paint?

It is generally admitted that prehistoric art was inspired by magic and that, in fact, the art stemmed from religious beliefs. This opinion is strengthened by the prehistoric pictures that adorn the walls of caverns in France and Spain, deep and dark caves that seem to be real sanctuaries. There can hardly be any doubt that the wizard of the *Trois-Frères* cave and the headless bear of the Montespan cavern must have had some magic character. Art for art's sake did not exist in those days; such a conception of art must have been the invention of men on a higher plane of cultural evolution. Still, this general rule must have had exceptions for certain of the subjects painted or engraved by the prehistoric artists have (at least as far as we can see) no mystical signification at all and indeed appear to have been the products of pure imagination and individual fancy. To tell the truth the two phenomena ('religious' art and 'art for art's sake') may well have existed side by side, though discussions as to the real 'significance' of prehistoric art (and the most fanciful hypotheses have been put forward) have been endless and no doubt will, in the future, cause a great deal more ink to be spilt.

I tackled this problem more than once when all the Tassili paintings were spread so lavishly before me. I kept a sharp lookout for what might be considered sanctuaries, but I must admit that what I discovered was not conclusive. The pictures had been painted here, there and everywhere without any apparent order, and it was only in very rare cases that any clearly magic character could be discerned.

The deep shelters such as those of Tan-Zoumiatak, Tamrit and Aouanrhet (these latter we examined later on) are no doubt those which may convey an impression of being sanctuaries. However, the subjects which can be seen there are the same as those visible in much smaller shelters where they are spread on the walls without any sign of special arrangement (and indeed in the greatest confusion). One is forced to be very prudent about making any pronouncement on this whole question—as far as the Tassili is concerned.

The fact is that the men of the Tassili painted everywhere they found a favourable spot and they painted most of all in the places where they lived. Most of the pictures, in fact, are in the homes of the ancient inhabitants of the plateau. The long shelters offered the artists ideally suitable surfaces and these are covered with frescoes; moreover, as there was plenty of room the figures stretch out one after the other and over-painting is uncommon. In the deep shelters, on the other hand, where the rock-walls' surface is restricted in area, there is plenty of over-painting to be seen, since space was soon exhausted and the men who inhabited the caves at different epochs systematically painted over the works of their predecessors.

However, we met with paintings in isolated niches, too, and these seemed to have no connection at all with living sites, so that it is impossible to lay down any hard and fast rule.

When it comes to determining if these pictures had or had not a magical character I must make it clear that the variety of our discoveries was very great. Among them can be distinguished at least sixteen phases (marked by different styles and corresponding no doubt to different epochs), each one of which has its own special characteristics. No doubt we did find human figures which must represent gods or wizards, but there are also assemblages which, it would seem, were painted by artists gifted with a rich imagination, men who made pictures for the simple pleasure of reproducing what they had seen with their own eyes and as they had seen it.

All this, I think, applies (although one must be very cautious) to the paintings of the period we called 'Bovidian', that in which the domesticated ox appears, and pictures of this phase occupy a very considerable place in the Tassili art; in fact, as far as mere numbers are concerned, the pictures with cattle occupy the first rank.

This phase is the most recent of the sixteen to which I have alluded, since the representations of oxen are often superposed upon the paintings of other epochs, but the 'Bovidian' phase is, all the same, earlier than that with pictures of horses for these latter are not prehistoric at all.

The favourite theme of the 'Bovidian' artist is, of course, the ox, reproduced in thousands of figures on the rock-walls and generally in large flocks led by cowherds. These cattle pictures are of remarkable artistic quality; the forms are copied directly from nature and painted with an evident and very skilful care for detail —horns, ears, hooves and tails. The bodies are shapely and perfectly natural, while the blotches on the hides are marked—most often in white. In fact, these paintings make up a polychrome art-phase in which red ochre is the predominant colour, but in which yellow, greenish and even blue pigments were employed.

Altogether we examined several hundred frescoes which can be assigned to this phase. Many were very similar, but each differed in particular details or took some slightly different form.

Curiously enough, and exceptionally among prehistoric painters,[1] the 'Bovidian' artists engraved their pictures before they painted them. I found many sketches which, by the multiplicity of the lines they show, suggest that these drawings were 'trial-pieces' comparable with those of a modern draughtsman or designer. The lines were very fine as though they had been incised with a flint-point. Many of the figures thus engraved showed a partial filling-in with ochre.

The human figures, in very varied costumes, also offered most attractive forms full of well-balanced elegance. Most of the attitudes suggested movement. You could see men in athletic poses drawing their bows at game or clashing in combat for the possession of flocks and herds or, again, joining in the dance.

Representations of household duties were also numerous and presented a very vivid picture of the domestic life of the ancient

---

[1] I have left this statement as the author has made it, but perhaps it will not be generally accepted that such engraving was altogether exceptional.

Tassilians. These lived in conical huts. The women crushed grain on quern-stones and rode straddle-back behind their men on the oxen. The whole economy was based upon oxen, but these people also possessed sheep and goats.

Were these people Negroes or 'whites'? The profiles were astonishing in their diversity. Some were prognathous, others of 'European' type, so that perhaps we may conclude that the physique of this people was not uniform and that several different human types lived side by side—just as do today the Tuareg and their Negro slaves.

The variety of costume (which included long tunics, short loin-cloths, garments of fibre, etc.) tends to confirm this assumption. All the same, the most common profile suggested that of Ethiopians, and it was almost certainly from the east that these great waves of pastoralist immigrants came who invaded not only the Tassili but much of the Sahara. The 'Bovidian' populations (who seem to have practised an ox-cult, as is indicated by an attribute sometimes seen between the oxen's horns) were, most probably, at one time in contact with Egyptian civilization. Moreover, in five different places we found on the frescoes representations of Egyptian-type Nile barges—a significant feature which seems to confirm the eastern origin of the 'Bovidians'.

There must be a special Providence that watches over archaeologists; anyway, that is how I would explain the presence of a heap of ashy matter against which I stumbled one day on the floor or a painted shelter. This heap was nothing more nor less than the remains of the old 'Bovidian' herdsmen's repasts. From a mass of pulverulent humus made up, apparently, of cow dung mixed with ash, I drew forth a number of bones among which were a great quantity of oxen ribs and teeth. There were also stones that had been used to triturate grain, stone axes, bone points, fragments of pottery and little pierced discs which the old Tassilians had cut out of ostrich eggshell in order to fashion necklaces, some pendants and also schist rings. There were even bits of the various-coloured ochres that were the raw materials of their pigments.

During the course of our expedition I found no less than five deposits of the same sort and with similar objects. Thanks to these we are now pretty well informed about the cultural level of these pastoralists. The charcoal recovered from these heaps will, we hope, give us, when it has been subjected to radio-carbon analysis, a dating for the deposits.

What, however, is already certain is that the herdsmen occupied the central Sahara at a time of considerable humidity, since in the frescoes are to be seen also elephant, rhinoceros, hippopotamus and giraffe. All such animals, as well, of course, as the oxen, needed plenty of water to drink and plenty of grass to eat. We made also another discovery of importance. In a small shelter some two thousand feet above sea-level, in the Aouanrhet massif (the highest in all the Tassili) we found on a rock-wall the picture of three reed canoes that seemed to be circling round three hippopotamuses.

But my luck did not hold right till the end, for I found nowhere the smallest fragment of any human skeleton, nor any monument or ancient tomb near the painted sites. So far we have no information as to how the Tassili prehistoric men buried their dead. Furthermore, nothing but the discovery of skulls could enable us to fix their exact racial grouping. But we must not give up hope of one day coming across such human remains.

Jebrin could not understand that, in the past, water must have filled the *wadis* and grass have covered the rocks and stones scattered about us. Where could so much water have come from? How could such grass have grown? His imagination could not stretch so far. Since his earliest infancy he had seen nothing but sand and stones in the Tassili. Moreover, as his father and grand-

17. Tamrit, The Stripped Tarout. The man to be seen in the photograph is the guide Sermi

18. *Timenzouzine: Human Figure with Body-Paintings: Bovidian Period*

19. *Timenzouzine: Elephant Engraved on a Rock: Bubalus Period*

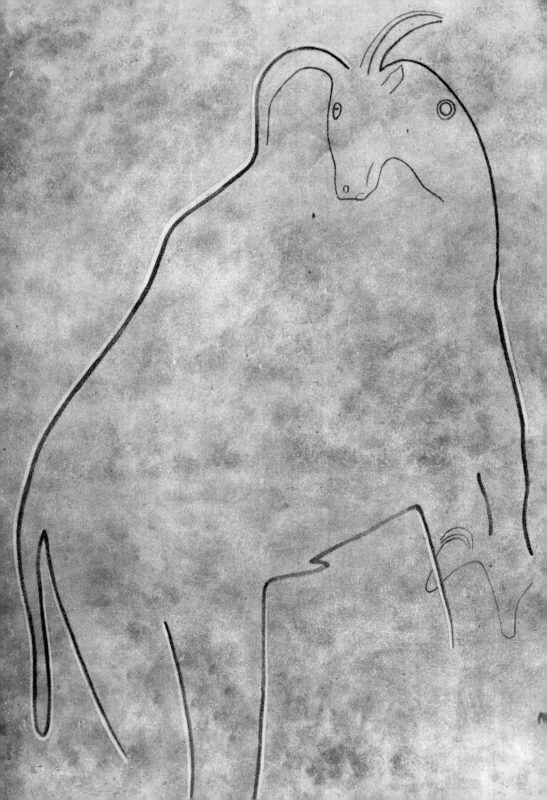

father had also seen nothing else, for Jebrin his country must always have been what it is today. After all, I am inclined to imagine that not a few French men and women reason in much the same sort of way.

The desiccation of the Sahara has been explained in the light of many hypotheses, but, as I have already stated, this drying up has not been accounted for in a satisfactory manner. It is in connection with this problem that the evidence of the cattle pictures is so significant, for we are surely justified in thinking that the presence of oxen must have been fatal to the vegetation. We can, indeed, see today in the Sudan steppes how the vegetation fades away in areas where herds of cattle graze. It is possible, in fact, to measure the spread of desert conditions by comparing such areas with check enclaves whose access is forbidden to the nomads. Herdsmen have ever been the great destroyers of vegetation and if we admit (as the evidence of the Tassili paintings suggests) that thousands of oxen wandered about in the Sahara for thousands of years, we may well assume their destructive action to have been so great that it contributed largely to the desiccation of the whole region. It would, of course, be absurd to regard cattle as solely responsible, climatic changes being the prime cause, but they played no small part.

What happened to these herdsmen and their cattle? Did they disappear without leaving a trace? It would surely be most improbable that such large numbers of people faded out completely. Rather, we may think that, goaded on by increasing drought, they sought out new pastures in the Sudan steppes to the south of the Sahara. In that region today there live three groups of pastoralists with their oxen—the 'Moors' (of Mauretania), the Tuareg and the Peuls. It is probably among these latter that we should seek for the descendants of our ancient Saharan cowherds, since oxen were adopted comparatively recently by the 'Moors' and Tuareg whereas

E

20. *Jabbaren. Antelope with an Elephant's Body.*
Decadent Period of the 'Round Heads'

tradition attributes to the Peuls the actual introduction of the ox into West Africa. Furthermore, in many of the painted scenes with human figures that date from the 'Bovidian' epoch, not a few of the graceful head-dresses remind one of those to be met with among the Peuls to this day.

6

Jabbaren with its Five Thousand Figures

COLONEL BRENANS, my old Saharan companion, whose premature death robbed our expedition of a fund of valuable experience, said to me a few weeks before we set out, 'Wait till you see Jabbaren; you'll be thunderstruck.'

Jabbaren? Just a little sandstone massif emerging, like so many others, modestly enough, from the Tassili plateau, but in an area where, at the foot of the rocks, erosion has scooped out deeper shelters than elsewhere. It was in 1938 that, led by our indefatigable Jebrin, Brenans discovered, and then copied, some of the splendid pictures on this site. It is one undoubtedly destined to become world-famous as soon as the copies we brought back with us are widely known.

After a month's work, and with all the elements leagued against us, we had finished copying the Timenzouzine paintings. At the last minute, indeed, a violent storm had almost destroyed, in a few seconds, the fruit of several weeks' intense labour. It was Irène Montandon who saved the situation, for she gave instructions just in time for all the copies to be rolled up and stowed away, together with the cameras, spools of film and sacks of flour, in a niche high up on the wall of the cliff. The rain fell heavily and resoundingly on the stones, and streamlets formed in the *wadi* near where our camp was pitched, but luckily enough no real damage was done.

From Djanet, where I happened to be, I gave orders to move to Jabbaren, a day's march off. But Irène left us to go to Paris where she had to sit for an examination. She took with her those copies which were finished and stored them away in safety. Claude told me later that, in accordance with Tuareg custom, they had all accompanied her for some distance on her journey. When the time came for saying good-bye they could not conceal their emotion, and old Jebrin, who had got used to the young woman's company and who used to converse with her in Tamashek—the Tuareg dialect of the Berber language—had tears in his eyes.

A new phase began. The drawing-tables, the folding ladders, the cases with the cooking utensils and the food supplies were once more hoisted on to camel-back. Then, under Jebrin's leadership, the caravan spread out over a desolate plateau. At last Jabbaren appeared at the bottom of a depression. Jabbaren is an assemblage of sandstone domes that remind you very much of the round huts seen in Negro villages. Nothing very exciting at first glance. Indeed, the place seemed to lack colour, but as soon as we had made our way into the sandstone formations, cries of admiration burst from all of us, so wild, so impressive, so majestic was the chaos of rocks. The 'huts' (formed by rocks eroded at their bases) offered the finest shelters we had as yet seen in the Tassili. The whole of the site constitutes a veritable 'city' with alleys, cross-roads and squares. Moreover, the walls are covered with hundreds of paintings executed in the most varied styles. We settled down, and in view of the immense amount of work in front of us, split up into two teams so as to save time in coming and going. Gianni, Jacques, Jo and Galigala took over the upper area, while Claude, Philippe, Rissa and I, as well as Jebrin and the Tuareg cameleers, made our headquarters in the lower area. We found little caverns in which we could camp and we hid our fruit juices and films in the cool holes of the rock-face. For the first few days, however, we tended to lose our way in this labyrinth, but we soon became familiar with the lay-out of our prehistoric city. We gave the streets names. There was the 'Jo Camp' and the 'H.Q.' (my own camp); farther off was 'Crocodile Alley', then came 'Giraffe Street', 'Aard-Vark Cavern', 'Viper Crossroads' (where Galigala killed a viper the day we arrived), 'Little Rabbit Cliff', and so forth—they were nearly all names chosen with reference to the paintings we discovered. In fact, the 'city' for so long deserted and silent was filled with surprising bustle and activity.

In the Tuareg language *Jabbaren* means the 'Giants' and the name refers to the prehistoric paintings, some of which depict human figures which are, indeed, gigantic in size. One of these figures, in fact (it is in a deep shelter with a concave ceiling), measures some eighteen feet high. No doubt it is one of the largest prehistoric pictures to be discovered up to now. You have to stand back so far in order to grasp the painting as a whole that we did not realize what it depicted until we had passed before it a number of times. The outline is simple, rather unskilfully executed. The head is round and the only feature it presents is a double oval in the middle of the face; in fact, the whole thing is very like the pictures we sometimes see of 'Martians'. 'Martians'—that would make a good heading for a sensational newspaper article, but it would have to tail off into an anticlimax, since if 'Martians' ever set foot in the Sahara it must have been a very, very long time ago, for these round-headed figures are, as far as we could make out, among the oldest in the Tassili!

'Martians' are common enough at Jabbaren, and we cleaned several fine frescoes datable to the 'Martian phase'. Brenans had noted several of such paintings, but the best of them seem to have eluded him, since they are, to all intents and purposes, invisible to the naked eye and are revealed only after prolonged sponging down with water. This method of wetting the frescoes allowed us, I would mention once more, to make discoveries of the highest importance. If it is practised with care such sponging down is very efficacious. We were able not only to remove from the ochres the layer of clayey dust that covered them, but we were also able to heighten the tints and thus restore them to their original vividness; hence the fresh appearance of our copies which has so much struck, I am told, those who have looked at them. During our cleaning operations we were to note, also, although all the ochres were perfectly indelible, some of the white pigment was much less fast.

Jabbaren is a world in itself. There are more than five hundred subjects in a quadrilateral that measures hardly more than six hundred yards on each side. If we base our calculations on the different pictorial phases represented we have to conclude that more than twelve different cultures succeeded one another at Jabbaren. Such a state of things is unique and Tassili must be held, for its size, to be the richest storehouse of prehistoric art in the whole world. The ground of the shelters in which we lived was covered with traces left by the troglodyte artists and their contemporaries. There were literally thousands of bits of pottery, hundreds of grinding stones, as well as stone pounders and strikers. Many lay as though they had only recently been used. Fossilized bones strewed the ravines where they, as well as flint arrow-points and stone axes, had been swept by the waters.

However, the greatest of the rupestral painted complexes are due to the 'Bovidians' and there are oxen everywhere. They are of all sizes and they are executed in a number of different styles. The beasts are presented in every possible position. The aesthetic quality of the execution is remarkable and the lines of exquisite delicacy. It was at Jabbaren that I noticed the 'Bovidians' engraved their pictures before they painted them. Of the same art-phase are the superb representations of giraffe, elephant, antelope, wild ass, goat and domesticated sheep. The most impressive of the frescoes shows a hunting scene, very powerfully realistic, and comprising no less than a hundred and thirty-five figures. Hunters armed with bows are chasing gazelles and antelopes. The centre of the picture is occupied by a wounded rhinoceros on the point of charging and losing blood from his nostrils. In one corner a group of archers is getting ready to attack a number of oxen while the cowherds are facing up to the challenge. The total surface of this painting is over twenty square yards and there can be no doubt that, of its sort, the picture must be considered as one of the finest in all pre-historic art. Five of us set to work to copy this fresco. We had to use our ladders, for the top figures are more than twelve feet from the ground.

Among the paintings of the phase of the Round-Headed men (the 'Martian' type) we also came across extraordinary figures such as an antelope with an elephant's body, over six feet high . . . prob-ably some divinity of those far-off times. Each day brought fresh surprises. All the walls of the Jabbaren shelters are covered with pictures and as many different levels are indicated by over-painting; these can, by comparison, be classified in a relative dating system. Thanks to the establishing of such a relative dating it may be possible one day to recognize and determine the origin of the artistic influences represented in the various phases. We shall know then who the ancient populations of the Sahara were, what was the part they played in the peopling of Africa, and these are things which we should never have been able to understand were it not for the discovery of the Tassili paintings.

Jabbaren was also to offer us, among others, a surprise that was of capital importance. While he was swabbing down a wall Claude brought to light four little figures of women with birds' heads, figures which were identical with some of those which are to be seen on ancient Egyptian monuments. The figures were, indeed, so characteristic that we expected to find a hieroglyphic inscription explaining the scene, but our hopes were vain. We found nothing of the kind, despite repeated washing of the surface.

But that night at camp the conversation was lively and my companions bombarded me with questions. Could it be possible that the people of the Pharaohs had pushed as far westward as the Tassili?

The answer I felt I had to give was this: if similar figures were to be found in very great numbers throughout the Sahara, then we might reply 'Yes'. But up to now nothing of the sort has been discovered. Our little goddesses with the birds' heads must belong to an historical period, maybe that of the eighteenth or nineteenth dynasties, and so, approximately, to 1200 B.C. We know that at this time the Libyans of the Fezzan (a region contiguous to the Tassili) were constantly at war with the Egyptians. Indeed, the Libyans attempted to conquer the Nile Valley. It is possible that the Egyptians sent out punitive expeditions into Libyan territory and pursued some Libyan detachments right into their refuge of the Tassili. That is not impossible, though it must remain doubtful whether the Egyptians could operate, in a hostile land and so far from their bases, when their lines of communication could hardly have been well assured. In any case, no Egyptian chronicle we know of makes any reference to such an expedition.

How then can these little goddesses be explained? There are two fairly plausible possibilities which may be considered. First that the artists were prisoners of war, or Egyptian travellers carried off to the Tassili, who there were inspired to paint by the surrounding pictures. Second, that the artists were Libyans who had lived in Egypt (freely or as prisoners) and were influenced by Egyptian culture to such an extent that, on their return home, they carried with them the art of the Nile Valley. Furthermore, centuries of almost uninterrupted struggle between Libyans and Egyptians might alone explain the penetration of Egyptian art far into the Sahara. The researches we hope to undertake in the future will provide, possibly, other and decisive evidence which can be used by those Egyptologists who study the problem.

While Claude was enriching our collection with these ravishing little bird-headed goddesses, Le Poitevin's team cleaned the walls of the Aard-Vark cavern. Here a dark patch had attracted our attention, but it was so shapeless that at first it was thought the thing was one of those paintings which are so much destroyed as to be practically unrecognizable. But once again swabbing produced marvellous results. At the third washing there appeared in all its beauty the large figure of a kneeling woman, nearly six feet in height. Her head was leaning against her flexed arm. Her face, with its elongated eyes, had a classical purity of line that recalled classical Greek art. The diadem that surrounded her head suggested that she was a personage of high position, maybe even a Libyan goddess. The features, in any case, were those of a woman of Mediterranean type.

When I was confronted with this painting my mind went wandering back to the stories about Antinea, the famed Libyan deity that inspired Pierre Benoit's novel—Antinea whom, it is said, the Greeks adopted under the name of Athene.

One curious detail, the Libyan goddess's hand is draped with a veil whose extremity is knotted in a fashion adopted by the Tuareg women of today when, as a choir, they sing during marriage festivals. Just a coincidence? Still, the connection between Tuareg and Libyans is today too widely accepted for me, at least, to deny that some link of relationship is indicated by this similarity.

For three whole months we came and went in Jabbaren, we moved our drawing-tables from one shelter to another, the boys and the Tuareg searched for wood and water, while Jebrin's camels made off calmly to the neighbouring pastures and the little asses trotted down with our mail in the direction of the Aroum Pass. The Tuareg of the region came often to visit us; they were attracted by the prospect of a good dish of noodles or couscous—the classical North African dish of semolina more or less seasoned with meat, raisins, etc.—while there was a continuous procession of children looking for jam or cakes. Such humble dainties made them so happy that we easily pardoned them their importunity, especially if one remembers that these young people spend their days hunting lizards and small rodents for their daily fare. At Jabbaren the children were always there to scrape the bottoms of the bowls and to make a few pence by selling us dolls made of camel-dung wrapped in rags. Since I gave little presents each time I was brought a polished stone axe, the more intelligent of the brats set about manufacturing such things with bits of schist or with pebbles found in the *wadi*. And I must admit that these imitations were very good indeed. Although these visitors made our camp lively enough they also threatened to reduce almost to nothing our already very scanty food reserves.

On two occasions, indeed, we were just about to give up our work because of lack of water. The pond that was full when we arrived had dried up during our long stay. But the Providence of archaeologists was on our side. At the very moment when, sick at heart, I was about to give orders to strike tents, black clouds gathered about us, a violent wind blew up and half an hour later a torrential rainstorm burst upon Jabbaren. In no time our camp was transformed into a swamp and the *wadi* overflowed its banks. Then our wood supply began to fail us. For three months we had burned *tarout* logs from old, dead tree-trunks we found round about, but at last there was no more wood. Finally, after a short respite, it was lack of water that made us move on. All the pools for a radius of some fifteen miles had dried out. For the last few days of our stay at Jabbaren we drank filthy mud scraped up from the bottom of the water-holes.

So we had to get back to Djanet. We collected our baggage, we folded up our tables and ladders, we loaded the beasts amid the cries of the cameleers. The gods of Jabbaren, the 'Bovidians' and their herds, the little Egyptian goddesses, transferred on to rolls of paper, went off on their way to the Museum of Man in Paris. Silence descended once more on the age-old alleys which, for three short months, had started into life. It was a silence of death that nothing would disturb for a very long time.

7

The Sanctuary of Aouanrhet

WHILE we were on our way down from Jabbaren my mind went back to Brenans and what he had told me. True enough, we had been astounded to discover so many marvels, but, no doubt, poor Brenans himself would have been very surprised had he known that well within sight of Jabbaren, on the other side of the *wadi*, the Aouanrhet cliffs hid masterpieces as strange as those we had seen already.

To tell the truth, so attracted were we by the delights of Jabbaren that we almost missed the sanctuary of the 'White Lady' of Aouanrhet. It was the arrival of the hot weather, and Guichard's taste for travel and also my old habit of interpreting in my own way the rather subjective reports of our friend Jebrin, that put us on the track.

From our look-out post at Jabbaren we commanded a view of almost all the eastern part of the Tassili and we had, before our eyes, a panorama of a peculiar sort that comprised a large depression.

The Oued Amazzar which, in the past, carved out a deep bed in the sandstone mass, occupies the bottom of a broad valley of V-shaped section, and this is exceptional since almost all the *wadis* of the Tassili lie at the bottom of canyons with practically vertical sides. No vegetation save for a few acacias and some tufts of *shebrok*. But above this monotonous view the landscape had a noble appearance. Both to the right and the left stretched a row of huge rocks grouped in compact massifs reminding one of oblong casemates made for giants.

I had prospected all the Oued Amazzar and the massifs along its sides as far as Ouan Abou. But what I had not explored was the rocks just opposite Jabbaren on the other side of the *wadi*. Jebrin had investigated this massif and had reported to me that he had there noticed several 'insignificant' paintings.

So I set off with Letellier to carry out a little reconnaissance farther away towards Tamrit, and told Guichard, who wanted to stretch his legs and get away from his paint-brushes for a time, to go and check, on the spot, what our old guide had told us.

This was a lucky idea of mine for when Guichard got back to camp he said that he had seen three interesting frescoes which he thought worth while copying.

As the Jabbaren job was coming to an end, I left Jo and Violet to finish the copies they had begun in the upper part of the Jabbaren massif, and went off with Guichard, Letellier and Jebrin to take up our quarters on the opposite side of the *wadi*.

The Aouanrhet massif is a real eagle's eyrie. It towers right up above Jabbaren and must stand at nearly six thousand feet. Aouanrhet is most difficult of access. The two camels and the two donkeys that carried our equipment struggled painfully on the slippery scree of the slopes. Jebrin, who had acted as guide to all the visitors to the Tassili, told me that we were the first Europeans to set foot there.

As soon as we had chosen a camp, we set off to make a systematic exploration of the rocks. In a shelter that was deep and quite dark I saw, first of all, two human figures with round heads; the paintings were in white pigment and were executed in a style that reminded me at once of that of a female figure in ochre we had copied at Tan-Zoumiatak. One of the two figures was quite clear and must have been about four feet eight inches high. I could make out the profile, lightly sketched, and as always in the 'Round-Headed' subjects, small and pointed breasts—for this picture represented a woman. However, what especially attracted my attention was a curious piece of over-painting on the left that covered the upper part of a second figure. This painting (the basic colour of which was brick-red ochre) depicted a man with a curiously striped body and wearing a mask. The very elongated face rather reminded one of a stylized antelope's head. Under the horns there bulged out a voluminous cap or bonnet. The ears, shown in profile, were barred with two parallel lines. It struck me at once that similar masks are to be found to this day in West Africa. In fact, when, later on, I undertook a search in the collections at the Museum of Man, I was not a little astonished to find that masks of a sort very similar to this shown in the fresco are still today in use among the Bambara or Sienuf people of the Ivory Coast, who employ such masks in initiation ceremonies.

This strange figure of Aouanrhet presented other curious features: the legs, which were straddled, as those of a man on horseback, and then the spreading flowers, rather like tulips, which sprang, stemmed, from the arms and thighs. I had already noted similar ornaments on a figure in the large shelter at Jabbaren, a painting I had called the 'Paunchy God' and in which I thought I could make out negroid features. And I remembered, also, that when I had seen the plants that seem to grow out of the 'Paunchy God's' body I had been reminded of some primitive divinity, a deity of the soil, master or creator of vegetation, such as is often enough to be found in the folklore and beliefs of the people inhabiting the Sudanese bush.

So my intuition seemed to be confirmed. This typical mask revealed, in unexpected fashion, though without any sort of doubt, that Negroes, in past ages, really had inhabited the Sahara, and also that in neolithic times masks had played there the same role that they do today in the animistic cults of the primitive societies in West Africa.

Here, then, was a discovery of some considerable significance and one that not only revolutionized what we know of the Negroes and their art but one which also must very keenly interest Africanists. It may be easily imagined then that when that evening I got back to camp I was full of excitement. The rest of our team had not been idle either, and I noted that they had been careful enough of their comfort to build up round our messing plot and our respective sleeping-places little walls of stone to protect us from the wind.

Anyway, our stay at Aouanrhet was a very pleasant one. Despite the late season—we were in June—the weather was spring-like. The air was light and the temperature very mild. And all this was a welcome change from Jabbaren, where sandstorms had bedevilled us almost every day. Unfortunately, however, there was no water and no wood near the Aouanrhet pictures so that we had to undertake long and wearisome excursions to find these indispensable supplies. The Aouanrhet massif is so denuded of vegetation (although we did discover three wretched little stunted and stripped wild olive-trees) that no Tuareg ever camp there nowadays. Only a few mouflon hunters venture into these wilds. Two at least of these wild sheep had, before our arrival, been living among the rocks, but they must have made off when they scented us. I was able to follow their quite fresh tracks for some distance in the direction of Idjefan.

While I was copying some very fine frescoes (of 'Bovidian' date and representing giraffes) near our camp, Guichard went off on a prospecting trip to the other end of the mountain mass. But he was soon back. He had discovered, so he told us, a curious figure. His description was, indeed, so interesting that I set off with him at once, my water-can and sponge in my hand.

The picture was in an isolated rock-shelter. Here again swabbing produced a magical effect. Claude, who was dabbing the surface bit by bit, watched me out of the corner of his eye so as to see how I was reacting to the revelation.

'Astounding!' I shouted, giving him a hearty slap on the shoulder, for what we saw was just that.

On the damp rock-surface stood out the gracious silhouette of a woman running. One of her legs, slightly flexed, just touched the ground, while the other was raised in the air as high as it would normally go. From the knees, the belt and the widely outstretched arms fell fine fringes. From either side of the head and above two horns that spread out horizontally was an extensive dotted area resembling a cloud of grain falling from a wheat field. Although the whole assemblage was skilfully and carefully composed there was something free and easy about it, something that was especially marked in the thin filaments depending from the hand coverings, and in the arm-band fringes waving, you would say, in the wind. The impression of movement was the further accentuated by the presence of little superposed human figures, dating no doubt from the 'Bovidian' epoch. These latter were in two groups, one set above the other, and each composed of six or eight individuals marching in Indian file. The contrast is striking between their contorted attitudes and the harmonious picture from which they stand out. These figures are, moreover, rather faint, for the red ochre in which they were executed has faded and, for a moment, I even thought that they were transparent.

The body of the woman, delicately painted in yellow ochre and outlined in white, is covered from the shoulders to the belly, at the base of the back and on the breasts with curious decorative designs, parallel rows of white spots enlivened with red lines. I have no doubt that this fine painting belongs to the style of the Round-Headed Men. The rounded belly, the convex, curved

21. Jabbaren. The 'Great Martian God'.
Decadent Period of the 'Round Heads'

22. *Jabbaren: Archer with Plumed Head-dress: 'Round Heads' Period: (Evolved)*

23. *Jabbaren: The 'Little Devils': 'Round Heads' Period: (Evolved)*

24. *Jabbaren: Fresco of the Little Archers: 'Round Heads' Period: (Evolved)*

25. *Jabbaren: Filiform Dancers: Uncertain Period*

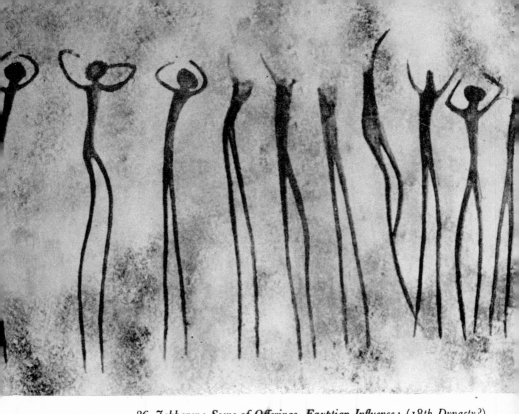

26. *Jabbaren: Scene of Offerings. Egyptian Influence:* (18th *Dynasty?*)

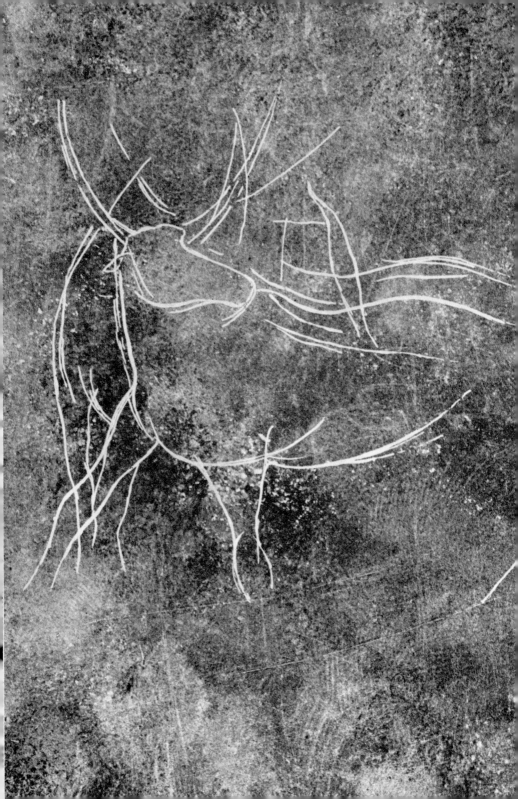

31. *Jabbaren: Archer from the Great Hunting Scene: Bovidian Period*

32. *Jabbaren: The Small-headed Woman: Bovidian Period*

33. *Jabbaren: 'Antinea': Post-Bovidian Period with Egyptian Influence*

Preceding pages:

27. *Jabbaren: Engraved Cattle: Bovidian Period*

28. *Jabbaren: Polychrome Cattle: Bovidian Period*

29. *Jabbaren: Cattle and Human Figures (engraved): Bovidian Period*

30. *Jabbaren: The 'Judges': Post-Bovidian Period with Egyptian Influence*

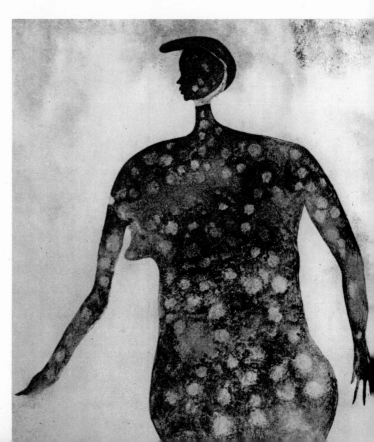

buttocks, the breasts like goat's udders all bear witness to a relationship with the old negroid stock whose characteristic features we had already encountered in many of the paintings at Tan-Zoumiatak and other places. The dotted lines must represent scarifications such as are still practised by the peoples of West Africa. Still, it seemed to me that in this Aouanrhet painting I could make out another artistic influence to which, for the moment, I did not dare put a name.

Guichard was sure that the fresco represented a goddess. In any case, it was the most beautiful, the most finished and the most original picture we had found among those executed by the 'Round-Headed Men'. First of all we called her the 'Horned Goddess' but, later on, by a comparison with the famous 'White Lady' of Brandberg, so dear to the Abbé Breuil[1]—a comparison which, of course, must be taken as referring only to artistic quality—we called her the 'White Lady' of Aouanrhet.

Was she a goddess? Well, that is not impossible, for this female figure, so carefully adorned, could hardly represent just a pretty girl of the time. Maybe she was a priestess dedicated to the cult of some agrarian divinity . . . this at least is suggested by the field of cereals above her horns.

In other paintings found a few days later in the same massif we were able to discern, from some characteristic features, an indication of Egyptian influence. Such features are, no doubt, not very marked in our 'White Lady'; still, all the same, some details such as the curve of the breasts, led us to think that the picture may have been executed at a time when Egyptian traditions were beginning to be felt in the Tassili. And when one thinks of Egypt one is reminded at once of Isis, who, with Osiris, was credited with having introduced agriculture into the Nile Valley . . . but

[1] The 'White Lady' is in the Maack Shelter, Tsisab gorge, in the Brandberg massif (South-West Africa).

F

34. Jabbaren. The 'Peul' Girls. Bovidian Period

we must leave such matters for Egyptologists to deal with. And, moreover, it is not the 'White Lady' alone that presents such problems. Other figures, indeed, are to be seen on the same rock-face: a kneeling woman, a man blowing a trumpet, a number of agile little people climbing up a tree and, finally, here is the prize piece . . . a big stylized fish displaying decoration identical with that on an Egyptian vase recovered from El Amarna and dating from the time of the Middle Kingdom.

This was not all. We were still to discover, quite near our camp, strange paintings whose meaning, once again, appeared to be explicable only in the light of religious themes typical of Egypt. One of these pictures represented a woman with an elongated body, exaggeratedly long limbs and giving the impression of floating in some liquid substance. With her long arms stretched out behind her she was pulling along a man, apparently lifeless, and doubled up. Lower down, on the same painted surface, a kneeling figure, bent forward, appeared to bear no relation to the 'floating' woman, neither did another figure walking with the upper part of the body also bent forward. However, a fourth figure, in white ochre, and in the same style as the 'floating' woman made a curious pendant to her. This fourth figure was that of a man emerging from an odd-looking, ovoid object which, from its colour and its internal construction, was something like a cross between a cockade, a snail and an egg! This obviously allegorical picture might represent birth while the upper painting might depict the voyage of the dead as imagined by the ancient Egyptians. However that may be, still, the red caps which, in these frescoes, cover the heads of the human figures, are exactly similar to those we observed in other Tassili paintings where Egyptian influence is obvious.

Egyptian traditions, then, and also negroid ones, and 'Bovidian' too. So we may explain, in part, the complex and original styles which are to be observed at this Aouanrhet site.

On the same rock-wall where we found our 'swimming woman with breasts on her back' and our 'snail man' there is a woman with tattooed breasts. She wears a red cap and is related both to the 'White Lady' (by the artistic style and by the tattoo marks) and to swimming-woman and snail-man assemblage (by the red caps). I may add, in passing, that André Vila, a member of my second team, showed me later on, in Paris, a photograph taken by him among the present-day 'lobi' and showing scarifications identical with those on this Aouanrhet figure. Maybe some parts of Black Africa have not changed very much during the last sixty centuries or so.

But our Aouanrhet discoveries did not end here. I will mention (out of the order of the finds and just to stress the great variety of subjects) a group of huts, an enormous animal looking like some aquatic larva, a fight among archers, persons with round heads accompanied by an elephant, a vegetable figuration representing probably a baobab-tree, a hunting scene with hippopotamus, oxen and so forth.

The paintings which we copied at Aouanrhet did not, it must be admitted, equal in number those at Jabbaren or even at Timenzouzine. But most of the Aouanrhet pictures are of rare quality and have a novel character that is especially interesting.

It is, also, strange that we should have discovered so many splendid paintings in a massif so difficult of access and so little suited for human habitation. The 'Bovidians', whose pastoral way of life compelled them to keep to the valleys and to high ground that was accessible to their animals, also visited Aouanrhet, but the 'Bovidian' paintings there are not numerous. Only a few commodious and comfortable shelters—where we found an abundant pottery—offered conditions of life which were acceptable to them.

As for the peoples who preceded these 'Bovidians' we may well ask ourselves, in view of the character of their art, whether they did not make Aouanrhet a high place for religious initiation and for secret, mysterious cults. This supposition appears plausible enough when one stands on the threshold of some of the shelters.

When, later on, we called to mind our stay at Aouanrhet it was the word 'sanctuary' that occurred to us most frequently.

8

A Saharan Summer

IN SPITE of some fatiguing days, and even some hours of real hardship at the end of our stay, we all retained marvellous memories of Jabbaren—this miraculous citadel of the pre-historic Sahara. All of us? Perhaps not the Benjamin of our party, Philippe. His unfortunate adventure is, maybe, worth relating as showing not only how careful we had to be, but also as indicating the rapidity and the suddenness with which the Sahara punishes the slightest imprudence however harmless it may seem in the eyes of the inexperienced traveller.

We had just settled in at Jabbaren and one of our main problems was that of establishing communications with Djanet. We were only about a mile and a half away from the Aroum Pass, so, at first sight, things looked simple enough. All the same, the pass had the reputation of being very difficult to negotiate. Philippe, whose job as photographer left him, at this period, with a good deal of spare time on his hands, was a robust young fellow and he did not, I must say, hesitate to help in anything where his muscular strength was needed. So, as I wanted to know what really were the conditions in the Aroum Pass—and how long we must reckon for getting through it—I decided one morning to send Philippe on a reconnaissance trip. The old saying is that the Sahara belongs to those who get up very early and I told Philippe to take off at daybreak, but he liked the snug warmth of his sleeping-bag. Moreover, at the last minute, Sermi, on the pretext that he was too tired, refused to go along; the result was that Philippe set off rather late. Still, as he had only two and a half miles to cover, all told—one half of which, however,was on a steep slope covered with rubble— he should have been back by noon; but at two o'clock there was still no Philippe. I thought he had been tired by the great heat and had found himself a place in the shade for a few hours; I did not, therefore, worry very much. About three o'clock, however, Jacques came running up to the camp in a state of great alarm. Philippe had just been found, apparently dying, about five hundred yards away from the shelter where Jacques and Jo were working.

'Wounded?'

'No, no.'

'What then? What's happened?'

Dying just because he had walked two and a half miles, even in the great heat; that just did not make sense. I went off and found Jo administering solicitous and apparently efficacious treatment, putting wet towels on Philippe's head and body and giving him little sips of water to drink. Philippe was lying on the ground, his arms spread wide apart and, to all appearances on the brink of heart-failure, nevertheless his pulse was quite regular. Slowly he came to and told us what had happened to him. He got down the *akba*[1] all right, but, as the heat became more and more intense, he could not resist emptying his water-flask. In so doing he committed his first and most grave error, for one must always keep a little water in reserve until one gets to the next water-hole. So, when he had to make his way up the pass again, it was getting late. The sunlight filled the gorge and the air was as hot as in a furnace. In such circumstances, the prudent thing to have done would have been to take shelter between two rocks and there to

[1] An *akba* is the slope up a pass.

wait for the heat of the day to abate. But Philippe, who was beginning to feel hungry, made up his mind to push on. He was only 500 yards from the camp when all his strength left him and he collapsed, though he just managed to yell out for help. The fact was that, in spite of his healthy and vigorous appearance, he suffered much from the heat during the summer and finally he had to ask to be sent home.

A little later on another adventure, also at Jabbaren, almost did for the whole team. Gianni, very exhausted and suffering from water on the knee (which had been aggravated by a fall he had sustained), came back in pretty bad shape from Djanet. His appetite was poor and the unfortunate fellow was quite obviously getting worse and worse every day. So I decided to send him back to Djanet and wrote off to Captain Rossi asking him to meet Gianni at the foot of the pass. The meeting-place was agreed upon and we all walked with Gianni as far as the beginning of the slope. Philippe and Galigala, with water-bottles on their shoulders, were to help Gianni down and were to await the arrival of the 4 × 4.[1] But Gianni, instead of taking with him just what was needful for the journey, insisted on removing all his baggage, so that, in the end, Jo and Claude also had to go down with him.

Jebrin and I walked back to the camp, but by nightfall no one had returned. At first I thought that the lads had taken advantage of the opportunity and had made a trip to Djanet. They would be back in the morning . . . and, indeed, when I woke up I found Claude and Jo sleeping heavily. When they woke up, however, what they had to tell had nothing to do with any jaunt to Djanet. Getting down the pass had been terrible work and the heat terrific. Gianni, who was not very steady on his legs, fell down three times. His bad knee began to pain him very much so that the march was slowed up considerably. Without bothering about the fact that

[1] A four-wheel-drive type of French car used in the desert.

they had but one water-skin for six people (for the brother of the boy Rissa had joined up with them at the last minute), they drank copiously despite Claude's warnings. When the party got to the bottom of the pass the skin was empty. They made their way to the place where the car was to meet them and then settled down in the shade of a rock to eat their midday meal. Their throats, by this time, were parched and they listened eagerly for the sound of a motor. Then everything seemed all right. But only for a few minutes. The sound they heard was that of the aeroplane that carried the weekly mail from Djanet to Ghat. At six in the afternoon, still no car, though it had been promised for four o'clock. What should be done? Gianni wanted to push on to Djanet at all costs. Philippe and Jacques suggested that all the party should go with him, but thirst is an evil counsellor. No agreement could be reached; each one put up a scheme which the others would not accept. The sun sank behind the Admer *erg* and still the five young men had seen no car. Had the captain forgotten them? Had we mistaken the day? The situation was decidedly unpleasant, to say the least, since, however welcome might be the cool of the evening, how was it possible for them to do nearly twenty miles on foot when they had not drunk anything for six hours and they felt themselves absolutely dehydrated?

Jo and Claude finally decided to walk back up to the camp as they thought it right I should know what had happened. Therefore, with Galigala, they set off up the pass while Philippe and Jacques with Gianni between them headed for Djanet.

Claude and Jo managed, without too much difficulty, to cover the two miles which separated them from the base of the pass; still, they were tortured with thirst and the going became more and more painful. Furthermore, it was by now pitch dark. After having clambered up several hundred yards they spotted a tiny

35. Aouanrhet. The Horned Goddess or 'White Lady'.
Period of 'Evolved' Round Heads. Egyptian Influence
36. Aouanrhet. The Swimming Woman with Breasts on her Back.
'Post Bovidian' Period with Egyptian Influence

flat space and slumped down there, where they remained in considerable discomfort until moonrise. Now, after having suffered all day long from the heat, they were tortured with the cold, since, of course, they had set off very lightly clad. They huddled up against one another, they were parched with thirst, they were racked with fatigue and, of course, sleep was impossible. Their tongues, which seemed to have swollen up, hurt them terribly. The strong taste of salt in their mouths was a constant torture. In fact they felt all the symptoms of advanced dehydration and feared that they would soon collapse.

I had myself experienced all these symptoms in the Hoggar years before and had been saved at the last moment only by the unexpected arrival of a Tuareg hunter.

A few hours more and all that would have been discovered would have been a corpse with pallid lips and a mouth full of sand and hands clutching at the earth—the last movement which the delirious traveller makes in an effort to scrabble for water. . . .

Once the moon was up Jo, Claude and Galigala continued their climb. With their tongues swollen and sticking to their palates, they stumbled on, not speaking a word but grabbing at the rocks and every moment stumbling against the stones. Luckily for them the obstacles were now clear in the moonlight but still the men had to clamber on and their legs were as water. Their sandals cracked and split. Like sleepwalkers they botched up their sandal-straps while around them the appalling majesty of the gorges glittered cold in the harsh moonlight. For a moment their artistic sensitiveness was aroused by the play of light and shade in the indescribable chaos of stone and rock. They could not tell me how long they spent getting up to the top of the pass. They took some courage from the fact that the camp was only about a mile and a half off . . . and then at five o'clock in the morning they could at last quench their thirst. The water of our pool seemed to

7. Aouanrhet. The Negro Mask. Period of the 'Round Heads'
nterior to that of the 'Decadent Styles'

them marvellously good. Still, a horrible feeling of thirst and a nauseating taste of salt bothered them for days after. However, for them at least the adventure was over.

What had happened to the others? Well, they were just as parched with thirst, but they had the advantage of a much better track since the terrain between the Aroum Pass and Djanet is just one long unbroken *reg* from which project, here and there, enormous tusks of granite. About eight o'clock at night a light pierced the blackness and the men heard the sound of a motor. An hour later they were safe and sound in the Djanet officers' mess, where they were able to recover from their fatigue. What had gone wrong? Just this, the order had been given to send off the car, but the order had not been executed, and Captain Rossi, astonished at seeing no one arrive, made enquiries . . . to learn that the 4 × 4 had not left Djanet.

Gianni was taken to hospital, where it was found that he had lost nearly forty pounds in weight. There was no question of curing him at Djanet. A week later he took the plane for Algiers and Paris.

Before we had left Paris, eight months before, I had told the members of the team that we were going to lead hard lives. They were all volunteers and enthusiastic at the thought of the adventures which lay before them. However, enthusiasm on the pavements of Paris is one thing, and enthusiasm after months of hardship and fatigue is another thing. 'The team spirit,' I told them, 'must always prevail in the country we are going to visit, a land where difficulties of all sorts will crop up every day; life in common will, no doubt, give rise to tension, even to quarrels; that's inevitable. But all that must be overcome; we must never lose sight of the fact that the enterprise must succeed and that, at the end of the expedition, we must find ourselves more united than when we started. We shall have been tempered by trials.'

What sort of life did we live near our shelters? Well, it was more or less the life of the men whose frescoes we were copying. It must not be forgotten (and the anecdotes I have just related give point to this) that the essential virtue in a Saharan is the ability to get along with very little. With experience, indeed, you realize that the key to success is conformity, as close as possible, to the mode of life of the Tuareg. That is to say, make do with the strict minimum necessary for what has to be done. How else, indeed, can one behave in a land to all intents and purposes devoid of resources and where the transport of anything from one place to another raises problems which are not, it is true, quite in-soluble, but which are nonetheless very difficult to solve?

I have already mentioned the hardships occasioned by the transport of supplies and equipment, the incidents and the acci-dents by the way, the tiresome and fatiguing portages up the passes where there was plenty of opportunity for breaking one's back. For these reasons, among others, our meals were appallingly monotonous.

Our boys, Rissa and Galigala, did the cooking and neither of them, needless to say, had ever studied in a school for hotel-keepers. Often, for some reason or another, we were obliged to prepare our meals ourselves. I must say that the *cuisine* was not complicated. A few handfuls of noodles thrown into boiling water, a spoonful of margarine, two cans of preserved meat—and that was all, the classical *shorbah*[1] of the Saharans. Turn and turn about noodles were replaced by coarse semolina (boiled as though to prepare a couscous) or rice or mashed potatoes prepared from desic-cated potato flour. We had sardines from time to time. Our dessert consisted of dry biscuits and jam—the latter always very welcome. We had as much coffee and tea as we could drink. To offset the lack of natural vitamins, we had vitaminized biscuits, almond

[1] *Shorbah* is the usual Arabic word for 'soup'.

paste, a little honey, and, above all, delicious fruit juices. The boys used flour or ground wheat to make bread. After dried yeast had been added, the balls of paste were cooked on hot cinders in an old saucepan turned upside-down. For some time, and while Irène supervised the operations, the proportions of yeast and flour, the time allowed for the dough to rise and that for the actual baking, the results were excellent, but after she left the boys got more careless. Often we had nothing to chew on but a soggy and insipid sort of paste.

Our usual drink was water—water that was often turbid, sometimes, indeed, really muddy and had innumerable little animals swimming about in it. Moreover, the water was, at times, made absolutely nauseating by a taste of rancid butter communicated by new water-skins.

We had not much time for amusement. As soon as the sun had risen we were at our work and we knocked off only at nightfall. We had, however, one day's rest, at Easter. Then a sheep brought to us by the Tuareg was slaughtered and we rejoiced.

Our only time for rest was in the evenings when we drank tea with the Tuareg. It was a time of silence when each of us drew on his pipe and puffed out clouds of smoke . . . after weeks and weeks of life in common we had practically nothing more to say to one another, except something about the work . . . each one of us had exhausted his supply of good stories. Some evenings, however, Rissa and Galigala danced to the strains of an aluminium flute through which Jebrin blew with some effort, though I must admit that the result was pretty satisfactory.

It is almost unbelievable how easily and quickly one can slip back into a primitive way of life. At first we arranged a sort of dining-room and kept to some of our civilized habits; we used knives, forks, plates and so forth. But once Irène had gone, half the utensils were discarded and soon we were eating in Tuareg fashion, that is to say helping ourselves with our wooden spoons[1] from the common platter. We drank from any sort of vessel and once our dish-cloths were worn out we used sand to dry the crockery. We paid no attention to whether the ground we ate on was scattered with goats' droppings or not.

Once the severe cold was over most of us abandoned our tents and slept at the back of the shelters. Very soon we were in a deplorable state; shock-headed, beards trimmed anyhow . . . our shadows against the grotto-walls stood out like the figures in a magic-lantern show . . . the Cave of Ali Baba and the Forty Thieves. Jo's beard grew so long that it made him look like an old sea-dog; moreover, it displayed a mixture of red, black and white hairs giving a most curious effect. Philippe, always ready to pose as the tough *hombre*, tried to sport a beard also, but the youthful fluff on his face gave him the appearance of a bearded woman.

As time went on our things were worn to shreds. Trousers, shoes and sandals were falling to bits. Claude lived for nearly a month in his pyjamas until one fine day they just split apart. Jo had to unsew his hip pockets so as to put patches on the seat of his shorts. Needle and thread soon held no secrets for us and we became expert darners. When the shoes we had brought with us were worn out we replaced them with Tuareg sandals made of bits of skins sewn one over the other and kept in place by a thong going between the toes and round the ankles. These sandals were very comfortable for walking about over the rocks, but we wore this footgear out so quickly that we could never get enough skins and had to walk barefoot.

Ablutions were reduced to the strict minimum. In very favoured spots where water was not too scarce it was possible to have a decent wash about one day out of three, but in the Aouanrhet

---

[1] Made for us by the Tuareg, for one fine day our knives and forks mysteriously disappeared. (Author's note.)

massif, for instance, where water was a day's march off, we had to do without washing for a month and a half. One day two of our team were seized with an altogether abnormal rage for cleanliness. Quite suddenly they washed themselves from head to foot; the Tuareg guides had beheld this strange sight, and one of them rushed shouting up to me:

'You know, those two over there they've gone absolutely raving mad.'

'Mad, eh. What's happened?'

'They're washing.'

He was quite indignant. And he was right. The next day, of course, all the water-skins were empty and a fresh water supply was due only in two days' time. We had to ration ourselves very strictly and we got no coffee to drink. However, generally speaking, we became accustomed to this lack of hygiene; after all, we were only imitating the Tuareg who never wash at all. They hold, indeed, that daily washing surely makes one ill and it is certain that in a climate so exceptionally dry as that of the Sahara the daily use of water on the skin provokes peeling. Thus the Tuareg rub their bodies with grease whenever they can get hold of any.

We were reduced, also, to adopting practices that were very much like those of the ancient inhabitants of the Tassili plateau. At one time, when we had run out of flour, we should have been at a loss what to do had we not brought with us from Djanet a little wheat. So, as and when we needed flour, we ground the wheat on a stone with a neolithic muller we found on the spot.

To sum up, it was a miserable enough life. Between the six of us, and during the first phase of the expedition, we lost more than eighty-eight pounds. This was the tribute privation and fatigue exacted from us. But we were free, absolutely free, with the superb feeling of freedom that is induced by vast horizons, pure air and a sky that was almost always azure blue.

9

From One Expedition to Another

EIGHT months of very hard work had, then, allowed us to make discoveries which revolutionized what had hitherto been known about Saharan prehistoric art. Moreover, we had been able to prepare an astonishing collection of copies. We might have been satisfied by such unexpected success, especially as we had gone far beyond the programme we had originally drawn up. I could have given orders to turn round for home. Still, I felt that when things were going so well we ought to finish off the job.

Then I thought of our departure from Djanet, of our painful ascent, with our heavy and cumbersome baggage, up to the Tassili and especially of the terribly fatiguing march up the Assakao Pass. There could be no question of taking down our tables and ladders and the rest of our things and then of bringing them up again six months later. For we absolutely had to come back, and come back as soon as possible, to continue the work that had been so successfully begun, but which was so far from finished—judging from what we had seen in many new shelters. When you have been absorbed in a task that has brought you much satisfaction, it is a good thing to realize that you are in duty bound to continue that task and to justify those who have put their trust in you, even if the effort you have to make reaches the very limit of human endurance.

Since Philippe and Jacques had decided to go back to Paris

(where, indeed, both of them were shortly to be called up for military service), I made up my mind to follow them and get together another team which would continue our work in the Tassili. Of the first team, which had explored the Djanet high plateau and had lived through the exciting adventures I have just described, only Guichard and Le Poitevin remained. They were to constitute the link between the first and second expeditions. Unfortunately, Le Poitevin, who had contracted a slight bronchitis by sleeping naked near an open window, had to stay in hospital for quite a long time. It was thus only our trusty Guichard who went up alone with Jebrin and the boy Mohammed. The three made their way towards the Ti-n-Tazarift massif where I had spotted many frescoes and where, consequently, there was a good deal to be done. The drawing-tables, the ladders and the cases of supplies were hoisted once more on to camel-back and once more underwent the rough treatment inevitable in a land of rocks and stones where moving about always presents troublesome problems.

During the first fortnight in October two resident students of the Abd-el-Tif Villa in Algiers came to join our team. Jack Chambrin and Robert Martin were two excellent painters who had already attracted attention by their original work. They were enthusiastic about our discoveries and wanted to get to know the Sahara. In fact they offered their help with the hope, also, of enriching their own art and experience in the company of prehistoric ancestors. In all this they were not disappointed, but camp life and our monotonous food were a great change from what our young men had been accustomed to in the comfort of Abd-el-Tif. Furthermore, the thermometer dropped day by day and the two, who had imagined they were going to stay in a tropical country, thought, after a few weeks, that they had got to the North Pole. The fact is that in December it is not at all hot in the Sahara, and at more than 4800 ft. up, where our camp was, a cold, often an

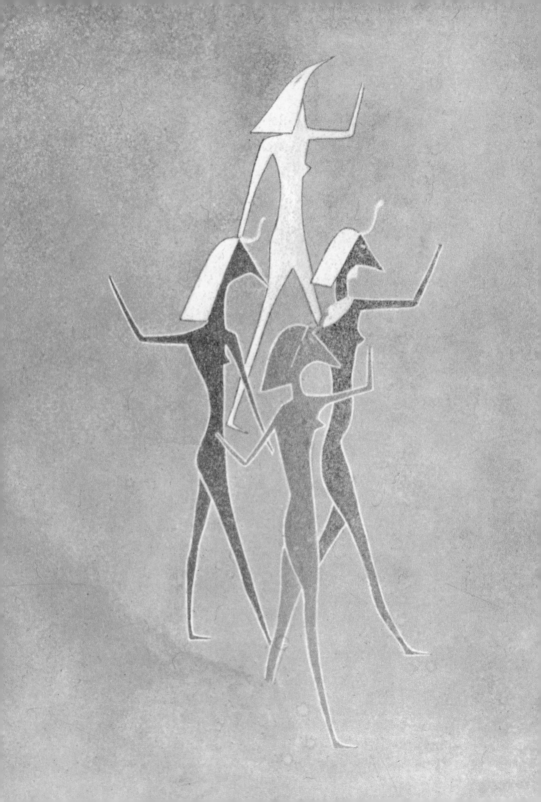

icy, wind whistled through the corridors and made our noses, including those of the camels, drip.

Working hours were, therefore, confined to those when the sun warmed up the air. But the days themselves got shorter and shorter. On 15th December ice appeared on the surface of the rock-pool and we had to break the crust every morning before we could get water for filling the skins. And these, one after the other, froze during the night and burst.

The *gouache* pigments assumed an unusual consistency and it became impossible to dissolve them. Moreover, how was it possible to draw and to paint with numbed fingers? The canned foods, though protected in cases, were affected. The green beans were congealed into blocks of ice while the tinned meat looked like frozen beef. The members of the team got out their padded jackets and their pullovers and, without much enthusiasm, faced up to the cold. Our native personnel were in still worse shape, for they did not know how to protect themselves against the weather.

First of all, it was one of Jebrin's sons, Matal, who fell sick—his father had brought him with him up to Ti-n-Tazarift. This fifteen-year-old lad was in any case far from robust and suffered from tuberculosis of the bones. We had to take him down to Djanet and put him into the infirmary. Then it was Jebrin's turn. His rheumatism was aggravated by the cold and soon crippled him entirely. He thought, indeed, that his last hour had come. He kept on shouting that he was done for and that we would soon have to bury him. However, he never quite lost his good temper and sense of humour. He burst out laughing when he showed us his poor legs, whose dried-up muscles were no longer of any use to him, and when he pointed to his skinny body and his knotted hands. Anyway, after all, life was like that; moreover, according to his own account he had enjoyed himself to the full. If Allah was calling him to paradise, well, he would have to die sooner or

G

*I. Jabbaren. The Bird-Headed Goddesses. Egyptian Influence.
18th Dynasty? (27 × 37 cm.)*

later, what did it really matter when? Moreover, henceforth he would not be able to run after the Tassili girls, the pursuit of whom had been for him, up to then, his chief aim and object in life.

When Jebrin decided to saddle his camel and go down to Djanet we were all persuaded that we should never see him again; indeed, we did not think that he would ever reach his destination. But he did get to Djanet all the same. His old carcass was tough enough . . . he joined his son in the infirmary.

Meanwhile life became every day more and more intolerable and work more and more vexatious. We had to make up our minds to pack our belongings and get back to Djanet. We were totally demoralized as a result of the great efforts sustained for months against all the elements combined and of the fatigue that had resulted from the immense amount of work done. On 20th December Chambrin left for Algiers. The remainder of the team, mounted on donkeys, got to Djanet for Christmas, just in time, indeed, to drink some champagne at the Christmas dinner. Then Le Poitevin took a plane for France.

After a few days' rest, however, Guichard and Martin went up on to the plateau again with the intention of finishing off their work. But wind and weather were too much for them. The cold was so intense that the two men had to keep inside their tents and snuggle down into their sleeping-bags from which they found it very hard to emerge.

All the supplies were put away in a small grotto and the copies of the frescoes in cases. As the two pushed their donkeys before them they were muffled up like Eskimoes. Their only thought was to get back to the Djanet mess.

'Oh, if we only had some booze,' groaned Martin, 'things would be a little better.'

Water flavoured with camel-dung was not the drink he had dreamed of when he set out on his Saharan adventure. Two months in the Tassili had completely disgusted him and, later on, at Djanet he was heard more than once to curse the entire Lhote expedition.

The little caravan sought refuge for the night in the shelter of a rock-cliff by the Tafalelet Pass. The men crouched round a wretched wood fire. The water-pot was set to boil so that the boy Mohammed could make hot tea—hot tea is good, very good, when the weather is cold. Then each one snuggled down as best he could into his sleeping-bag. Soon, in the moonlight there were only three dark blotches from which emerged sonorous snores.

Down from the sky, like a shower of stars, little sequins sparkled under the moonbeams, but no living thing that night put his nose outside his lair, not even the jackal, who kept to his hole in the rock, and still less the horned viper—so sensitive to cold—asleep at the bottom of some rodent's burrow.

When the men woke up under a dull grey sky, the ground was so white that they thought they were lying under some spotless shroud.

'That's it, white sheets,' murmured Guichard, who felt he must be dreaming, for ten months his only bed had been his sleeping-bag, which was pretty grubby by this time, it must be confessed.

And that happened on 6th January. It had snowed all night.

At the same time that Guichard and the others were living through a Saharan snowstorm, I was rushing about in order to reorganize the expedition with a view to further work on copying the Tassili pictures. I had, indeed, a few weeks before, left the Tassili for Paris, there to find new collaborators and also new backing for more action. Therefore, in that same month of January, a team of men was, in Indian file, climbing up the steep slope of the Tafalelet Pass.

Guichard, the only survivor of the previous team, was waiting for us at Djanet. In the eyes of his four young companions he was quite the seasoned Saharan.

Among the newcomers there was not one well-known artist; they were young men without any pretensions, but they did know how to use their paint-brushes. Let me introduce the new team.

Michel Brézillon, thirty-three years old. He came from the Jura and, so he said, was descended from the Mongols. Sure enough, some of his features did suggest such an ancestry. He threw up a very good job in order to join us. Long before, as a Boy Scout, he had been struck by the account of my Saharan adventures—heard one night by the camp-fire—and ever since that moment he had dreamed of such things for himself. A bookseller by trade, he had for some years managed the principal bookshop at Saigon in Indo-China. He had a remarkable degree of adaptability and his cultural background was sound, but nothing had seemed to indicate that one day he would find himself on the Tassili to copy prehistoric paintings. All the same, in his Indo-Chinese days he had daubed a few canvases which he had sold to the customers in his shop.

Michel was to prove to be an absolutely first-rate companion and, what is precious on an expedition like ours, a man full of common sense. He it was who, that day, marched at the head of the file. He was followed by a fat figure of a man hung about with a number of bags and satchels and wearing a remarkable linen hat which would have been more in place on the Canebière at Marseilles than among the Saharan rocks. André Vila was the name of this parasol-wearer. He was, by profession, a skilled craftsman in dental prothesis, but he was also an amateur photographer and a keen member of the Liotard group, a young offshoot of the Explorers' Club. Vila came from the Dordogne and had been brought up on food cooked in goose-fat—this possibly explained his healthy appearance. Needless to say, I did not want any dental prothesis done on the expedition, but it was as a photographer that Vila interested me. Still, as a photographer he might be superfluous, as I had just taken on a film-cameraman. I was much tempted to leave Vila in Paris, but he begged so earnestly to be allowed to come with us that I ended by yielding to his charm of manner. He was warned that he would have to turn his hand to any sort of work, and he agreed, with great good humour, to accept the most menial tasks.

The cinema man, J. D. Lajoux, had a good many more qualifications for he had been in the Army cinematographic service. He had shot a film among the Mois in Indo-China.[1] Moreover, he was as strong as a Turk, as dark-skinned and hairy as a Blackamoor, although he came from the Vosges Mountains. His head was harder than the Tassili rocks—if I assign to him the hardness of quartz (No. 7 on the Mohr scale), I am hardly exaggerating. Nevertheless, his food consisted mostly of milk, fruit juices, mineral water and sweets . . . but his head was so hard that one day, during some incident I cannot remember, maybe a case had slipped to the ground, Guichard's hand was badly bruised after contact with Vila's skull.

The fourth member of the team, a confirmed denizen of Montparnasse, was a 'real' painter. His style, he explained to me, was that of covering his canvases with little dabs of different-coloured pigments. This technique, as he was to find out later, bore no resemblance at all to that of the Saharan frescoes. Y.X., who had been at school with Lajoux, unfortunately could not stand the Tassili for more than three weeks. He had to be evacuated urgently to Djanet and then sent back to Paris. I mention him, therefore, simply to make the record complete. His case—which

[1] This film was shown at the Vienna meeting of the International Congress of Anthropological and Ethnological Sciences in 1952. (Author's note.)

was far from unique—just illustrates the fact that the Sahara is not the sand desert of Ermenonville[1] and not everyone can adapt himself to Saharan conditions.

This unfortunate incident deprived us of a painter and threatened to upset all the programme of our work. So I was obliged to telegraph in a hurry for a candidate who had been kept in reserve, since after the appearance of the newspaper articles, which reported our first discoveries, I got more than twenty applications from people who wanted to join us, and these came not only from France, but also from Holland, Belgium, Switzerland and especially from Germany—several of the latter were from women.

The new arrival, Jean Lesage, was by occupation a bookseller at Tarbes—you may begin to think that I recruited my staff mainly from bookshops—but he liked messing about with paints, he had done some cave exploration, he had an air pilot's certificate, so, after all, he was not such a bad candidate for membership of a Saharan expedition.

It was arranged that the Dodge from the *bordj* would take the whole lot to the foot of the Tafalelet *akba*. My camel also went along. Jebrin, in fact, was a great stickler for etiquette as understood among the Tuareg and he would on no account leave the animal behind since the chief must mount nothing else but a noble beast.

However, what Jebrin had not managed to do was to get together the six camels we absolutely needed to haul up our mass of baggage to Ti-n-Tazarift. So we had to have recourse to requisition, which was by no means easy. Each time a Tuareg came to Djanet with a camel-load of wood, Jebrin, who was on the

---

[1] The so-called *Désert d'Ermenonville*, some twenty miles to the north-east of Paris, comprises a portion known as the 'Sea of Sand'. It is a vast expanse of dunes and sandhills and one of the most strange areas in the Ile-de-France.

look-out, rushed off to the assistant officer of the Annex, who immediately ordered a *goumier*[1] to bring the beast in. In this way it took no less than ten days to collect six camels. During the whole of our expedition we were worried by troubles of this kind which cost us much time and money. We had to adopt similar tactics to get donkeys when we could find none on the spot; Agaoued, our head-man, had to go and look for asses in Tuareg encampments all over the Tassili.

There could be no question of sending the laden camels up the Tafalelet Pass, so Jebrin went off with one of his Kel Medak[2] friends by the Assakao Pass, and so following the track taken by the first party and making a long detour to reach Ti-n-Tazarift, where Jebrin's son Matal had stopped behind to look after our camp and our supplies.

We went on foot to the top of the first *akba* of Tafalelet, where I had arranged to meet Agaoued and his asses. First incident: Agaoued got late to the meeting-place and, thinking we had not yet arrived, stopped at the bottom of the pass. By ten o'clock at night we were shivering in the cold. We had no blankets or food, or wood to kindle a fire. We got so depressed and disgusted at waiting at the foot of high cliffs swept by an icy wind that Guichard, Brézillon and Lajoux decided to go down the *akba* and look for our people. The way was not easy by daylight, but on a dark night it was very disagreeable indeed, especially as we were still tired from our exertions in climbing up. So, for a good start, our new members were getting a taste of Saharan adventure. Still, the excitement of novelty gripped them and they faced up cheerfully to the extra effort demanded of them. Our new 'boys', however, did not take matters so light-heartedly, and when Guichard ordered them to bring up our sleeping-bags, a *guerba*[3]

[1] A *goumier* is a member of a *goum* (see p. 29).
[2] The Kel Medak (*see* p. 135) was Jebrin's own tribe of Tuareg.
[3] *Guerba* (French transliteration) is Arabic for a water-skin.

of water and a few foodstuffs, one of the men, absolutely disgusted at a beginning that boded no good for the future, just disappeared into the night without saying a word.[1]

The next morning Agaoued and his donkeys caught up with us at last. Then came the unending climbs between the second and third *akbas* of the pass. We were hemmed in by high cliffs which, on either side, overhung the track in the most impressive manner. We were making our way along a path that was thousands of years old, that had been trodden in distant ages by the hippopotamus and elephant hunters on their march to the banks of the great Tafasseset river, now but a fossil trench; a route taken by the herdsmen going to pasture their cattle on the Admer plain It is a track used for countless ages by those who have crossed the plateau between the two oases of Ghat and Djanet for peaceful or for warlike reasons.

The voices of our teamsters, as they urged on the donkeys, echoed in the canyon as in a cathedral. Every rolling stone made mysterious reverberations so that our new members, as yet unaccustomed to this strange scenery and these uncanny noises, fell silent overcome by a feeling of extreme foreboding. However, we arrived without mishap at the foot of the third *akba*. This slope was to remind all of us that a Tassili expedition is not child's play at all.

The pull up this *akba* is, in fact, one of the steepest in all the Tassili. Our donkeys recognized this fact straightway for they stopped and shot sideways glances at one another, glances that revealed apprehension and fear. Despite their reputation, donkeys

---

[1] The increasing difficulties we were to meet with in recruiting personnel were due to the prospection for minerals in the Sahara. The Edjelé oil-wells are only two or three hundred miles from the Tassili and the oil-men call on labour in the oases and especially in that of Djanet, where, on one occasion, 150 workmen were signed on in a single day. All the cooks, all the 'boys', are snapped up and get very high wages, at least twice as high as those ruling at Djanet, and also a number of additional advantages. The result is that the oasis is now drained of its best workers. (Author's note.)

II. Sefar. The Great God with Praying Women. Decadent Phase of the 'Round Heads'. (760 × 360 cm.)

are not at all stupid. They are, indeed, quite clever enough to realize what is expected of them, and they are also cunning enough to disappear when they feel some harsh task is going to be imposed upon them. Our beasts, as a matter of fact, knew the road quite well for they had been over it many times and showed no surprise at what lay before them. As they saw us behind them, they started off, as well as they could, up the incline, but they had not gone ten yards before the leading donkey halted and held up all his brethren, who were only too delighted at the delay. The path did not permit of two men going forward side by side and we had to perform all sorts of acrobatics over the rocks so as to get to the guilty party, who, after being well belaboured, started up again, trotting and jumping about on the rubble and stones as lively as a gazelle.

Ten times, twenty times, the same performance had to be gone through, but, finally, the beasts, worn out by their efforts, would not budge. Several, indeed, fell down and provoked dangerous little avalanches of stones. We must, at all costs, break the deadlock. Several of us tackled each beast; one pulled in front, the others shoved behind. All this, however, did not prevent more falls or the tail of one of the donkeys coming off in Vila's hands. In the rocky gully we could not get any fallen load up again on to the beasts' backs (as we had so often found to our cost), so we had to carry up the baggage on our own backs as far as the top of the pass. I shall not soon forget the sight of one donkey watching Guichard and Agaoued stumbling along under the weight of their burdens and winking at us as though to say, 'We've played a good joke on the two fellows who've been tormenting us ever since the foot of the pass.' And the ass clambered up the last slopes gaily enough, flapping his ears as he went. He needed no encouragement. When he got to the top he was so delighted that he staled on Agaoued's feet. Our chief teamster was furious at such a display of bad manners.

The climb up the Tafalelet Pass had almost done for our donkeys so that even after the halt necessary for readjusting the loads some of the animals still stumbled and fell. It was painful to see the vain efforts the poor beasts made to get up. Their muscles would knot under their trembling flesh and their breath roared like a bellows through their bloodshot nostrils. Most of them could not manage to stagger to their feet alone. We had to pick the stones from out of their hooves and then help them up. So, at the first suitable spot, we bivouacked for the night.

In fact, these Tassili passes gave us a terrible time, so that the prospect of having to get through a considerable number of convoys to supply us until the end of our stay was a dismal one and caused me much apprehension, especially as the Tuareg had more and more difficulty in furnishing the necessary pack-animals. The ideal solution, I thought, in a region so inaccessible, would be transport by helicopter or parachute. There was no chance of a helicopter for such planes are still very uncommon in the Sahara, but what about parachutes? I had just learned that an air squadron was to be based on Fort-Flatters, from which point aeroplanes would fly periodically both to Fort-Polignac and to Djanet. I resolved, therefore, to write a request to the Chief of the Air H.Q. in Algiers (with whom for years I had been on friendly terms), and I felt sure he would do his best to help us out.

During the night we all got back our strength. The donkeys were quite lively when we rounded them up in the morning, and remained passive while they were being laden. Our little caravan set off. I got astride my camel. He was an old hand at the Tassili country and had climbed up the various *akbas* without much trouble. It is true that he carried no burden.

On the Tamrit plateau we looked like characters out of the Bible. The camel leading, the asses and the men following might have reminded an onlooker of the Flight into Egypt or of a little group of Bedouin on their way to Bethlehem. The purring of an engine made us look up. Captains Rossi and Letellier were searching for us and trying to spot our encampment from a Junkers 52. But they did not notice us. After eight hours' march and a halt by the rock-pools, where each one of us washed, we finally got to Ti-n-Tazarift where Jebrin and his camels had arrived a few hours before.

10

The New Team at Ti-n-Tazarift

THE setting of Ti-n-Tazarift was perhaps the most beautiful of all those sites where we had stayed up to then. Never, in any case, did the word 'city' so well apply as to this sandstone massif, for its centre is marked by a huge amphitheatre with a diameter of more than five hundred yards. It looks like an immense public square with houses grouped round it and giving off from it avenues, streets, passages, even blind alleys. As at the other sites so at Ti-n-Tazarift; it was in the hollows at the base of the rocks that we found the paintings. Windblown sand had piled up in several of the corridors so that they were blocked with great dunes which, under the sun's rays, took on dazzling golden tints. This silting up certainly added to the picturesqueness of the site, but it was not long before we came to curse the masses of sand. For months we had to plough our way through a crumbling surface of quartz grains while the intense reflection of the sunlight half blinded us as we walked and, moreover, made the air in the corridors almost unbreathable. Our camp was set up in the shelter of a spur of rock and at about a hundred yards from a pool which supplied us with water. Our Tuareg found nearby a shelter where they were well out of the wind. Only the sounds of hewing of wood and drawing of water broke the immense silence of Ti-n-Tazarift, for there were no human inhabitants in the neighbourhood. We were alone with the rocks.

The 'city', for it is a real prehistoric town, stretches for some mile and a quarter. We had chosen to camp in about the middle of the site so that we could reach any point easily. Before I had gone off to Paris I had made a tour of 'my' property. I had visited corridor after corridor and had made a list of the paintings. What had struck me was that in the painted shelters at Ti-n-Tazarift there were no fragments of pottery, grinding-stones and mullers such as we had found at Jabbaren. Instead, axes chipped from large flakes, as well as big faceted stones bearing traces of percussion, lay everywhere.

It is true that at this new site we did not see on the walls those hundreds and hundreds of oxen which meet the eye everywhere at Jabbaren. Most of these new pictures belonged to the ancient period of the Round-Headed Men, men of the 'Martian' type. One of the strangest figures represents a woman on her back. She has a cylindrical body but no feet, her arms are raised and she is accompanied by two mouflon. Admittedly, the painting is not beautiful, but it is very impressive. Among other human figures, in the same art-style, are to be seen a giant archer and a man looking as though he were swimming. All this assemblage of Round-Headed men made me conclude that their culture did not include either pottery or grinding-stones or mullers, and that it must have been they who made and used the curious and primitively chipped stone axes whose presence had puzzled me for such a long time.

Another shelter's walls were covered with hands, one, at least, of which was placed over part of a 'Bovidian' style painting. Imprints of hands are found in many European palaeolithic grottoes and are considered to be among the most ancient of pictorial designs since they were produced by men who, in far-distant ages, soaked their hands in colouring matter and then pressed them against a rock-face. Representations of hands on rocks are to be seen in many different parts of the world and they are thought, generally, to have a magical significance relating either to an act of taking possession or to a rite for warding off evil spirits or, again, to one designed for arresting such spirits by mystifying them with the hands and thus neutralizing influences hostile to man.

In the Tassili sites we noted two sorts of hand imprints, one in outline and the other produced by application of powdered pigment. The first sort, which appears to be the more ancient, is in violaceous ochre, and is found associated with Round-Headed figures of the first phase. With the hand is seen also part of the forearm. The surface, within the outlines, is covered with geometric designs dividing the whole into a number of separate areas, the meaning of which is, of course, unknown to us. Although the painting is recognizably that of a hand it is not one of absolute fidelity to nature. The unnatural proportions of the fingers, for instance, indicate that they are freehand drawings.

The hands of the second type are quite different and these we found at Ti-n-Tazarift as we had at Jabbaren and Sefar. These hands are 'negatives' or stencils. The hand was placed against the rock-face and then pulverized white pigment was blown over it, so that the surface covered by the hand remains blank while all the surrounding rock is whitened. The outline, in this case, is, of course, quite faithful. What strikes you especially is the slenderness of the fingers, which often seem to be those of a woman. The significance of the stencils is a little less mysterious than that of the painted hands. According to the opinions now current among ethnologists, the hand stencils indicate a double rite, first that of pulverization through blowing (and hence some act connected with the breath and designed to ward off evil spirits), and second, the placing of the hand on the rock-wall which may indicate a symbolical taking of possession. To this day, in North African villages, a woman will impress her hand into the wet clay above the entrance of a house she is to inhabit. 'It brings good luck' is the usual explanation given by the mass of the people. The jewel called the 'Hand of Fatima' is only a stylized representation of such an imprint. It is certain that such customs are survivals of ancient and prehistoric magic rites.

The painted hands upon the rock-walls produce a strange impression. Their presence evokes, to a point of obsession, an atmosphere peculiar to haunted places or ancient sanctuaries. Here our far-off ancestors (as yet incapable of understanding even as much as we do of the real cause of things) and believing in maleficent forces of nature they were not strong enough to fight, attempted, by practices efficacious in their own eyes, to bewilder and avert the action of evil spirits.

We were all the more inclined to be impressed by the hands since the Tuareg around us still believed in the spirits of the caves, the winds and the waters.

The Assakao Pass, that we took on our way up to the plateau, is reputed to be much haunted by *jinnūn*, so our guides and cameleers never failed to place a stone on the large rock that rises at the entrance to the gorges. Such stones are offerings made to the genius of the place. There are thousands of similar sites in the Sahara of the Tuareg.

The foot, or the sandal, also plays a considerable part in Saharan magic. In not a few places, especially near difficult passages, you may see outlines of feet drawn upon the rock-slabs and these are intended to distract the attention of the evil spirits while the traveller himself makes his way peacefully up the pass.

The Tassili is a land of wizards, of witches, of enchantments. The women of Ghat have the reputation of being able to distil powerful love-philtres which hold a man fast. These are the famed *borbors* about which so much has been written. Their action tends to diminish a man's resistance so that he is the more readily at the mercy of a woman. If a man falls sick for no reason that is apparent to those around him, then it is said he has been 'borborized'.

According to a good many Frenchmen of the Sahara I myself have been 'borborized', and it was 'borborization' which was given as the explanation for the illness and death of the unfortunate geologist C. Kilian, today considered as the real discoverer of oil in the Sahara. Needless to say, neither Kilian nor I was ever 'borborized' by Tuareg women, though the story, ridiculous as it is, is still firmly believed in some quarters.

Divination is also much in honour in the land of the Veiled Men. No one sets off on a journey or engages in any important enterprise without consulting the 'viper that walks on the sands', for it will tell you whether good or evil will result from what you are about to undertake. Jebrin interrogated the 'viper' and promised us all sorts of almost incredible good luck . . . love and money. However, what interested me most at the time was to get an assurance that our expedition would go satisfactorily. Well, we shall see!

You will remember that the copying of all the many paintings at Ti-n-Tazarift had not been finished off by the Guichard-Le Poitevin-Martin-Chambrin team which had had to leave because the cold became so intense. There were still quite ten excellent frescoes to be dealt with, and they offered a good opportunity for showing the newcomers our methods of working and also for initiating them into the life of the Sahara.

Once the tents had been put up and the camp installed, there were no mishaps during the process of adaptation to novel conditions. The weather was spring-like and in no way to be compared with that we had had to endure twelve months before at the same time of year.

For the first time since we had arrived in the Tassili we saw some flights of locusts. The insects were not very numerous, but

III.   Jabbaren. Polychrome Cattle. 'Bovidian' Period. (152 × 105 cm.

they rejoiced the hearts of our Tuareg, who at break of dawn set out to catch the creatures on the trees where they had alighted. It was manna from heaven, for one and all of the inhabitants of the Sahara, whether they be Arab, Tuareg or 'Moor', enjoy a meal of fried locusts.

Matal and Agaoued, who had gone off to see the donkeys grazing, brought back one morning a sackful of locusts which they at once threw living upon the hot cinders. A locust, at least to our French palates, is not really what you would call a titbit, but for men who are always hungry and whose usual fare is lizards and small rodents, locusts make a very acceptable meal. When a locust is fried or grilled its legs are pulled off (for these are set with prickles), and as much of the wings as has not been consumed by the fire is also removed. The head is wrenched off at the same time and the digestive tube extracted for this is quite un-eatable on account of the green matter it contains. The rest of the insect is then munched much in the way that we eat shrimps. Sometimes the Tuareg reduce the grilled locusts to powder and place it in skin sacks (*mezwed*) so that it can be eaten, with the addition of water or milk, when the men are travelling.

I myself rather like locusts and at times have eaten nothing else for weeks, but I am free to admit that the taste is not to every-one's liking. It seems, however, that the really smart thing to do now in the Ouargla oasis—where the oil-men forgather—is to served grilled locusts (at five francs apiece!) with the *apéritifs*. Maybe a rather expensive bit of snobbery, but one that certainly does provide plenty of local colour.

All the members of the team wanted, of course, to sample locust. Each one of them gave his opinion. Michel Brézillon thought they tasted like cardboard. Vila compared them with nuts. Lajoux said they reminded him of grass. I maintained they had a savour of shrimps, while Guichard made a grimace and spat out

H

the insect after a vain attempt to swallow it. For him, it was for all the world like excrement.

We cannot argue, it is said, about tastes and colours, though, happily enough, our ideas about colours are not usually so divergent as our tastes.

While work was being pushed forward at Ti-n-Tazarift, I went on a reconnaissance expedition to Sefar, a massif about two hours' march away, where we had noticed numerous paintings, so I took the necessary steps for setting up our tents there. Jebrin had, at last, managed to get together half a dozen camels and as many asses. Once more came all the trouble of breaking camp, transporting our equipment and stores and setting up another encampment.

II

The Great God of Sefar

BEFORE we set foot in it the Sefar massif had never been visited by any European—though the legend is firmly rooted that the Sahara is all known and that there is no more exploration to be done in the great desert. Sefar is still more picturesque than Ti-n-Tazarift. The main axis of Sefar is a very deep canyon and the whole mountain mass is cut through with narrow gorges hollowed out of blocks of sandstone and bordered by columns which are sometimes gigantic in size. Moreover, Sefar is remarkable for its changes of level and these do not make getting about any the easier. Several amphitheatres—some of which are high up and, so to speak, suspended in the air—form as many different 'cities' with their main squares, their avenues and their narrow streets. Some rock formations are astonishingly like the temples of Angkor, while others remind you of Rheims Cathedral after it was bombarded in the First World War. Once again we felt ourselves ridiculous dwarfs beside giants in stone. Maybe it was all this that weighed down upon the spirit of Y.X., while the rest of us on arriving burst out into cries of admiration. Anyway, we shall never know, although it was at this moment that his nerves gave way and we had to take steps to send him home. Luckily, Guichard was due for a few weeks' leave, so they went off together. Naturally, then, the work progressed more slowly, and I began to ask myself, with some anxiety, if our programme for copying all the frescoes at Sefar could possibly be finished before the great heat of summer.

It was a heavy blow losing two of our party at once, but we all did our best. Furthermore, the new team, which had seen what had been done by the first, had from the beginning been determined to produce nothing inferior. Brézillon, after having worked under Guichard's guidance, had now found his feet. In a few weeks he had acquired a technique as good as that of any of us, and he could now tackle the most complicated paintings. One fine morning, Vila, who up to then had kept strictly to his own speciality, photography, had a talk with me. Since we looked like being held up for lack of artists, he said he was ready to set to work and see what he could do. Obviously this offer showed a good deal of temerity, but what I liked was Vila's evident good-will and willingness to help. So I took him in hand, gave him, first of all, easy subjects to copy, advised him and corrected his work when it was necessary. He gradually got the knack of the thing and rendered most useful service to the expedition.

The cinephotographer Lajoux was at first hardly more skilful at handling a pencil, but I took him on to help me. Between the two of us we made a considerable number of the tracings at Sefar, and we saved the painters a good deal of time since they found all their preliminary work was done for them.

There was no doubt about it. A spirit of emulation inspired the new team. Certainly, its morale was as high as circumstances demanded. In fact, the members of our party showed themselves fully up to the standard I had expected.

For all of us, Sefar was a source of great joy. If the number of pictures is not as great as at Jabbaren (still the real high place of Saharan prehistoric art), the quality and variety of the Sefar frescoes are such as to make the site of the very highest interest.

Once again we were confronted with strange figures—figures so different from those of what we may call 'classical' prehistoric art, that we felt we were moving about in a world that bore no relation to any other, a world apart. Yes, a world apart, for our discoveries opened up what were really quite new perspectives into Africa's past, perspectives which threw light both upon the vast range as well as the originality of Africa's ancient history. But the very abundance of the evidence raises as many problems as it solves. Unexpected links and relationships are evident, so that instead of isolated facts we have the beginnings of a connected story. We have still to fill in the details, however, and lengthy research of absorbing interest is necessary.

Discovery is, of course, excellent, but it is not all; we must interpret the discoveries, we must strive to understand them, we must solve the mysteries of the many different cultures whose art we can admire, we must endeavour to date these, place them in time and space, explain them. Such interpretation is very far from easy and is proportionately less easy as the number of different subjects and of various art-phases is great. Each of the sites we found offered fresh subject-matter for discussion, and by comparing the new data with that already established we obtained additional information which shed surprising light on such and such an art-phase.

In nearly all the frescoes there was some details which told us something, not only of the arts and crafts, but also of the religious beliefs of prehistoric men. From this it can be seen that the archaeologist works like a detective among the relics of the distant past.

At Tamrit and at Jabbaren we copied so many scenes painted by the herdsmen that the oxen ended by giving our artists 'indigestion'.

Indeed, if an artist has to copy the same sort of subject all the time he ends by being bored and stale—even if the oxen did show variations and differences to the extent that among the several thousand representations which figure today in our archives there are not two exactly alike. Sefar, however, was to provide us with some new information about the history of these cattle-breeders and pastoralists. We discovered some absolutely unknown and unrecorded scenes depicting not only domesticated dogs but also women doing field-work. Now, up to the time of these finds, we did not know when the domestic dog first appeared in the Sahara. We did know that such animals were kept by the horse-riding populations, but now, thanks to the Sefar pictures, we are certain that the herdsmen also had dogs, though of a species different from those of the horsemen.

It may be thought that this is a very small point, but let me say that it is just such details which allow archaeologists to reconstruct the past. Again, the presence of grinding-stones and mullers in great quantities gives us a pretty strong hint that these Saharan pastoralists also practised an agriculture, although it is true that these primitive utensils might have served to grind wild grains. However, the question is set at rest by the pictures we discovered of women working in the fields.

At Sefar we copied also dance scenes where the women are holding in their hands a sort of rattle while others carry what must be digging-sticks furnished with a ball-weight. Still further details, not before recorded, give us a clear idea of the life led by the Tassili herdsmen.

All things considered, the 'Bovidian' type scenes are much less numerous at Sefar than at the other sites. There is nothing to be surprised at in this, for after one has wandered about all over the Sefar massif, one realizes this is so jagged, so contorted and cut about that, with the exception of two or three valleys, where the going must have been fairly easy, the remainder was hardly access-ible to herds of oxen. This conclusion suggests that the herdsmen

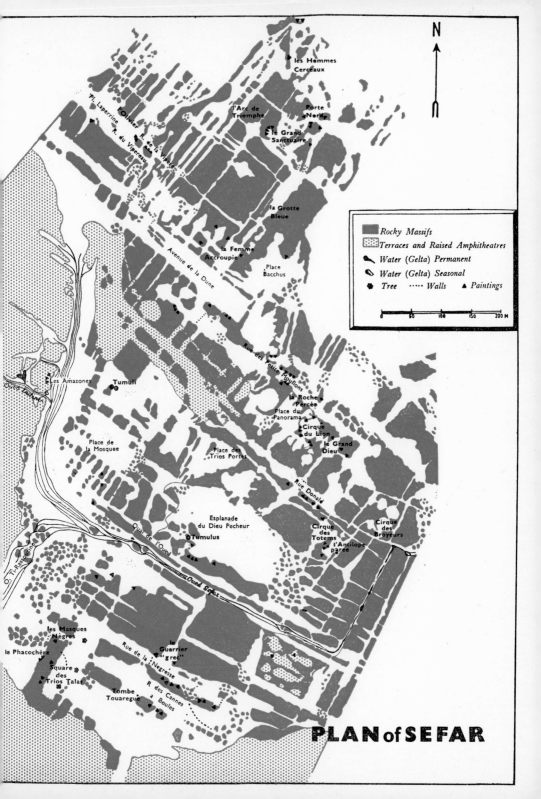

PLAN of SEFAR

painted, not where individual fancy led them, but in the places
where they stayed with their cattle.

The most remarkable of all the Sefar frescoes are those belonging to the 'Martian' group and comprising human figures—such
as we had already met with in abundance at Jabbaren—one of
which, over eighteen feet high, really astounded us by its huge
size.

At Sefar the figures were a little less large, but they did not
fail to make a great impression upon us by their strange attitudes
and by the well-chosen spots they occupy, so that the images loom
up in the most extraordinary way. In one of the first shelters we
explored such a 'Martian' figure stared down at us. It was over
eight feet tall. With raised hands and holding in them some unidentifiable ovoid object, he faced the light and lorded it over
about a hundred other paintings of various epochs. Many of these
paintings had been partially destroyed by water-action; still, we
could recognize among them, executed in the same style, women
of lesser stature who were raising their arms toward the giant as
though addressing some supplication to him. To the left, and in
the same technique, was a huge ox, nearly nine feet long . . . it
was the most imposing figure in the whole shelter.

But the entire assemblage is most impressive and the grandiose
setting provided by the overhanging cliff towering above added not
a little to our sense of awe. I do not think that I have ever felt, elsewhere, such a sensation of power and mystery. This being rose up
to his full height before us. We realized we were intruders profaning
a holy place, a temple erected to the honour of primitive divinity.
The figure had something so monstrous and inhuman about it,
that we baptized our discovery 'The Abominable Sand Man'.

But Jebrin, who was guiding us through the inextricable maze
of alleys, led us off to another amphitheatre quite near. Here
the impression of sublimity exceeded anything we could have
imagined. The principal place in the shelter was also occupied by

an 'Abominable Sand Man' exactly ten feet nine inches high, and in the same style as the first but better preserved. To his left, five women were walking one behind the other in a sort of procession. Their hands were raised towards the main figure, apparently in supplication. To the right was a large antelope in red ochre and a woman lying on her back. Her legs were apart and her belly so swollen that she seemed upon the point of giving birth. This scene certainly has a magic character connected with some fertility or maternity cult. The women, whose whole attitude showed clearly enough fear of, and respect for, the main personage, could only be praying to become mothers or to have an easy delivery. We were to find other praying female figures in other Sefar frescoes and we noted that such figures were almost always accompanied by representations of large animals, as for instance, in another shelter where the women are painted over an enormous feline—probably a lion—more than twelve feet long.

How were we to copy such scenes? The great adoration fresco alone occupied a surface of nearly thirty square yards. Still, obviously, we could not keep such a vision to ourselves. It is touching evidence of ingenuous beliefs—beliefs so deep-rooted in the heart of women that, to this day, we can sense the echo of them in some cults practised in Brittanny and other parts of France. So this gigantic fresco was photographed, filmed, traced and, despite its size, it may be seen today reconstructed in its entirety in the Museum of Man. This was not the only painting of its kind, for Sefar offers many other subjects of the same art-phase . . . quantities of human figures—many of them headless—animals such as elephants, large antelopes, giraffes, mouflon, warthogs and so forth.

The mouflon, especially, seems to have played an important role in the beliefs of the ancient Saharan populations. Pictures of this beast are to be seen in profusion on the painted walls of

38. *Aouanrhet: The 'Marathon Race': Post-Bovidian Period with Egyptian Influence*

39. *Aouanrhet: The Negress with Tattooed Breasts: Post-Bovidian Period with Egyptian Influence*

40. *Aouanrhet: Hippopotamus Hunt: Bovidian Period*

the Tassili and the animal appears in the most ancient phases as well as in the most recent ones. The wizard with mouflon's feet whom we had recognized at Timenzouzine had worn a dance costume and also a mouflon skin over his shoulders. We were to see, later on, drawings of mouflons' horns which would indicate the place this wild sheep must have occupied in the spiritual life of our Tassili painters. The mouflon is, of course, a dweller in the mountains and it is still to be encountered in the Tassili, the Hoggar and, indeed, in all the mountain massifs of the Sahara. It is an agile beast, full of courage, and as it has an extraordinarily acute sense of smell it is very difficult to approach. Among the Tuareg a gazelle hunter enjoys almost no prestige at all, whereas a mouflon hunter is regarded with respect. A whole folklore has grown up around this animal, its habits and its characteristics. It is even held that there are mouflon *jinnūn* that can lead goats astray, and even women.

Mouflon hunting is hedged about with an elaborate ritual Formerly the wild sheep were followed by dogs and then killed with javelins. Today shot-guns are more often used. But whatever may be the arms he employs, the Tuareg who goes off to hunt mouflon never tells anyone of his plans lest he draw down ill-luck upon himself. Some hunters, as they set off, put a stone on their heads and go forwards skipping and jumping while they recite, several times in succession, a secret incantation.

41. *Ti-n-Tazarift. Our Camp*
42. *Ti-n-Tazarift. The Archers. Bovidian Period*

12

The Ancient Route Through the Central Sahara

Our guide Jebrin was foot-loose. A long stay in one spot got him down, and if he had to look too often at the same scene he became depressed. In this, moreover, he was a true Saharan Tuareg, for these people, in their search for pasture, have to be continually on the move. So, as time went on, he came to talk to me more and more so as to find out how fast our work was proceeding. He made no secret of his keen desire to see us finish off as quickly as possible and then to move our tents to a fresh site. Several times he was astute enough to keep us in the dark about painted shelters quite nearby. However, as he soon found out, all his cunning was in vain, for we always ended up by finding them and in our wanderings about the Sefar massif very few paintings escaped us.

So, to kill time, he would disappear for a few days on the pretext that he had to go to prospect for water-holes, seek camels or beg for donkeys. When I saw that he had to be on the move I told him to visit the neighbouring massifs and make sure there were no pictures in them.

Through being with us he had acquired a good knowledge of painted shelters. He was as agile as a monkey, despite his age and his rheumatism, and he never shirked reconnaissance work. He would clamber up the most inaccessible heights and examine the rock-faces methodically and with great care. He never seemed to get tired even after scrambling about in the most difficult nooks and corners.

Many a time I was to note that he had been before me when I set off to explore some area. The traces of his sandals, clear enough on the sand, proved that he had examined the walls with great attention. All the same, there were at Aouanrhet some exceedingly fine frescoes which seemed to have escaped his notice, though it must be confessed they were not easy to see. Indeed, a thorough swabbing of the surface was necessary in order to bring out the colours. All the same, I rather suspected that Jebrin was keeping his own counsel, for he must have definitely disliked the idea of our settling on an eagle's eyrie most difficult of access and devoid of water, firewood or any vegetation at all.

Sometimes work did not keep me in camp. Then I would tell Jebrin to saddle our camels. He would perk up at once. Off we would go, just the two of us, and for five or six days we would seek adventure. It was during one of these excursions and while I was exploring the farther end of the Adjefou cliffs that I discovered a huge rock-face covered with paintings comprising a large number of human figures in red ochre and executed in a very peculiar style. The bodies were of what might be called 'bi-triangular' shape, the limbs were elongated and the heads represented by a little stick. These figures, in tight-fitting tunics, held in one hand a lance and in the other an object which looked like a little rectangular basket. This type of painting was not quite unknown to me, for there are some in this style to be seen in the shelters of the Oued Djerat, of Tamajert and of Tiror which I had visited in 1934. Similar pictures exist also in the Hoggar—near to the village of Tit—and even right out in the middle of the Tanezrouft, near the Ti-m-Missao well.

It is to this 'bi-triangular' style that the first paintings found in the Tassili belong. These are not, strictly speaking, prehistoric at all, since they constitute evidence for the arrival in the Sahara of a new human group accompanied by domestic horses (up to that time unknown in the desert) and war-chariots.

On the Adjefou rocks I remarked, indeed, two rather well-preserved paintings of the famous war-chariots which, of course, despite all my explanations, were quite incomprehensible to Jebrin. The chariots were not, however, any novelty in the Tassili since on our very first journey in the region we had copied eight of them, five at Ti-n-Bedjedj and three at Tamrit.

All the same, the chariots of Adjefou are peculiar in that they are the most easterly of any painted chariots discovered up to now —I would stress the word 'painted', for there are some representations of chariots still farther east, right in the Fezzan, but they are engraved on the rocks. These engravings were discovered by Italian archaeologists in 1933.

A little later on, during an exploration in the Ala-n-Edoument area, I was to discover another chariot painted in red ochre and kaolin. It figured, however, not in a warlike scene but in one of an antelope hunt. We were to see still more chariots at Tiror, at Tin Abou Teka and at I-n-Itinen on the track from Medak towards Iherir. This whole assemblage of war-chariot paintings is, as we shall see, of very considerable interest.

Indeed, the discovery of the first chariots provoked much excited discussion among archaeologists. Who could have drawn such things and what did they signify? Was it possible that once upon a time chariots had been driven through the Sahara? Herodotus mentions a people belonging to the great Libyan nation, the Garamantes (whose land lay in what is now the Fezzan), and they used in war two-wheeled chariots drawn by two or four horses. With these vehicles the Garamantes pursued another Saharan people, the 'Troglodytes', who lived in caverns and rock-shelters.

As Herodotus died about 425 B.C. the events he related would have occurred, then, in the fifth century before our era.

The Saharan chariot-pictures were thus, first of all, attributed to the Garamantes of Herodotus, but a careful examination of the paintings was made by such experts as Dussaud and Salomon Reinach, who concluded that the very peculiar style of the horses galloping with outstretched legs was one clearly related to the 'flying gallop' convention in the Mycenaean art of Crete.

Now, it is certain that, about 1200 B.C., immigrants from Crete landed in Cyrenaica with the object of conquering Egypt and that these people mingled with the Libyans. So it appeared that the Saharan chariots must be more ancient than had at first been supposed and that they confirmed what historians had called (borrowing the words of the ancient Egyptian texts) an invasion by the 'Peoples of the Sea'. It might well be that after the failure of their campaigns against Egypt these invaders of Cretan origin retired towards the Saharan regions, where, sooner or later, the 'Peoples of the Sea' became assimilated with their Libyan allies.

This whole problem had for long interested me, and I was able, during my desert wanderings, to identify chariots on several occasions. In 1935, when I was on my way back from Gao (on the Niger) and was crossing the Adrar of the Iforas massif, I noticed an engraved chariot near the Arli well, on the track from the Hoggar to Es-Souk—this latter place was the old Tademekka of the Sudanese Berbers.

The discovery was indeed an extraordinary one to make so far south. At once the idea crossed my mind that the chariot people may have driven right across the Sahara. Was this possible? Was it plausible? But to answer 'yes' on the strength of one single piece of evidence would have been rash indeed, and I was careful to hazard no theory at all.

I moved off towards the north, crossed the Tanezrouft and went to get water at the Ti-m-Missao well situated approximately half-way between the Adrar of the Iforas and the Hoggar. Ti-m-Missao is a point that all caravans must touch at on their way north and, indeed, it seems that they must have done so from very distant times since the immediate approaches to the well are covered with engravings, paintings and inscriptions of various sorts and of various ages ranging from that of the 'Bovidians' to that of the modern Arabic-speaking Moslem populations. Under a layer of inscriptions painted in Tifinagh[1] I made out five pictures of chariots.

The figures of the horses were, for the most part, obliterated, but the wheels and the drivers were still clearly visible. These chariots were of the same type as those of the Tassili. There could not be any further doubt. I was most certainly on the ancient road from the Gulf of Syrtis to the Niger river. Furthermore, if people with chariots had come to Ti-m-Missao that could not have been just by chance, for it takes six days' march over a desert *reg* to reach the well from the Hoggar, and that means there could have been no dawdling or detours. The goal of the charioteers must, then, have been the Adrar of the Iforas, maybe the old Tademekka, the only settlement in the entire region that was but six days' march from the Niger. All the same, there was a gap. At the time I am speaking of no representation of a chariot had been discovered in the Hoggar. So there was a blank on the archaeological map between the Tassili and Ti-m-Missao, and this blank prevented me from tracing out the probable chariot-route.

It took me no less than fifteen years to fill in this blank.

At I-n-Daladj, in 1950, right in the middle of the Koudia, at the highest point of the track which crosses the Hoggar from north

[1] Tifinagh is the peculiar script used to write the Tamashek dialect of Berber, that is, the Tuareg language. The use of Tifinagh is now almost, if not entirely, abandoned.

to south, I was able to copy from isolated stone slabs three pictures of chariots. A few days afterwards, at Hirafok, a small agricultural centre situated on the northern slopes of the Hoggar and rich in rupestral engravings, I made the discovery of two more chariots. Then, while I was prospecting the southern area of the massif I found more chariots at Tit and at Aguennar—ten in all. Everything was beginning to get clear. It was, in fact, now possible for me to plot out in all its length the track which for millenia had linked the Syrtis to the Niger. This route followed the most reasonable line, for it corresponded exactly with the ground usable by vehicles going over or round the mountain massifs at the most favourable point, avoiding the sand areas, and linking up with the essential water-holes, that is to say those which can be regarded as perennial.[1]

The geographical disposition of the painted chariots (which must be considered, as a whole, more ancient than the engraved chariots) shows that the horse-riding populations, descended from the 'Peoples of the Sea' and the Libyans, must have reached the Niger by almost as early as 1000 B.C. Such an idea quite revolutionized the theories formerly held, namely that the Libyan populations did not occupy the Sahara until a comparatively late date. Specialists in ancient African geography who took their stand on the texts of Pliny and Ptolemy thought indeed (and some of these specialists still think) that the 'Land of the Blacks' referred to by these authors was situated, not on the latitude of the Niger, but that it began on the edge of the North African cultivable areas, that is to say, roughly speaking, at the foot of the Saharan Atlas and the Aurès Mountains. It may, however, be suggested that

[1] Other representations have been discovered in the western Sahara where another trans-Saharan track (though later in date than that from the Syrtis to the Niger) seems to have existed. In 1955 I was able to copy, near the Oued Dermel, in the south of the Algerian department of Oran, no less than 110 engraved chariots on stone slabs forming the banks of the wadi. (Author's note.)

such an interpretation should be supported by clear archaeological evidence. But no material proof, no ruin of a village, no necropolis, no human skeleton which can be assigned to Negroes contemporary with Pliny and Ptolemy has ever been discovered in the area in question.

The pictures of chariots and of horsemen (these latter derived, some centuries later, from the chariot people) allow us to trace, by representations on the rocks of the Tassili, the Hoggar and the Adrar of the Iforas, the different routes of expansion towards the south and also from east to west—in fact on either side of the Syrtis-Niger route which appears to have been the main artery of traffic.

One discovery leads to another and often allows us to lift the veil from things which have been obscure enough. What I want to mention now is Roman penetration into the Sahara. The subject may seem to be rather alien to that of our Tassili explorations since it does not relate to prehistory at all. But why should we limit our exploration arbitrarily and exclusively to the Tassili? The thing to do was to take advantage of every opportunity and this is what we did, but not to the neglect of any archaeological problem. Of course, we might have had the luck during our wanderings to find an inscription or a stela of Roman date . . . but we did not. All the same, I examined the routes leading to the plateau as well as those on it because it is quite certain that some of them were followed by the Romans during the period (and even before the period) when the *III Legio Augusta*, stationed at Cydamus (now Ghadamès), had subjected the town of Rapsa (now Ghat), some fifty miles east as the crow flies, from Djanet.

We know for certain, from Latin texts, that two Roman expeditions penetrated pretty far into the Sahara. These were, first, that of Septimius Flaccus in A.D. 70 and second, that of Iulius

Maternus in A.D. 86. But we do not know how far they got. We may suppose, anyway, that these two expeditions were preceded by another in A.D. 19, when first Cyrenaica and then the Fezzan were conquered and Roman rule was extended to beyond Biskra in the Algerian south. This was the campaign of the legate Cornelius Balbus, and it procured for him when he returned to Rome a commander-in-chief's coveted reward, a Triumph. The tradition was that the chariot of the triumphant conqueror should be followed by his vanquished enemies and by bearers of standards on which were inscribed the names of the nations and the cities subdued.

Now, for the Balbus Triumph, these names corresponded well enough (at least partially) with the names of well-known places such as Thuben (now Tobna), Vescere (now Biskra), Tabudeos (now Thouda), Cydamus (now Ghadamès), Rapsa (now Ghat) and so forth. Others of the names had not been identified either because they referred to places which, later on, just faded away, and whose sites even have not been identified, or because the names have so changed in the course of ages, after multiple transcriptions and alterations that they are not now recognizable.

But the discovery of the chariot route seemed to me to open up new possibilities and I wondered if certain names of towns and regions conquered by Balbus, but not identified, might not be found along this route. It was, indeed, a great highway, cutting through the whole breadth of the Sahara from Phazania (that is, the Fezzan) to the Niger, and there were many indications that this track had been, in Roman times, a caravan route by which the products of the Sudan, gold, ivory, ostrich feathers and slaves, were sent to the commercial centres of the north where they found a ready market among the Romans. But had there not been also as before in the early times of the Garamantes, a military line of penetration?

I

So I set to work to reread the well-known text of Pliny relating to Balbus's Triumph. Great was my stupefaction to find among the places mentioned two whose names sounded familiar to my ears—Alasi and Balsa. The site of the well-known French military post of Fort-Polignac bears, indeed, in the Tuareg language, the name of Ilezy and it lies right on the Syrtis-Niger route, straight to the south of Ghadamès, and is linked to that oasis by the track that has now become celebrated as that leading to the Edjelé oil-wells. If the Romans, after having reached Ghadamès, pushed farther south, then they must, of necessity, have struck Ilezy. The slight difference in spelling between 'Alasi' and 'Ilezy' may impress us, but for a Tuareg there is no difference at all, since in Tamashek the consonants only are written.

The other name, 'Balsa', is, phonetically, so close to 'Abalessa' that there cannot, I think, be any doubt that the two names are one and the same, especially if we take into account that Abalessa is a small agricultural centre in the Hoggar and that it lies on the chariot route. Moreover, there is at Abalessa a little ruined fort in which have been found impressions of Roman coins bearing the image of the Emperor Constantine as well as a glass vase and Roman lamps.

No doubt this material is not older than the third century A.D., and the presence of these relics of Roman workmanship may well be explained by the commercial contacts which the people of the country must have maintained, as I have already said, with the Romans. But there was another possibility suggested by the probable identity of Abalessa with Balsa, and this was that the Romans themselves used the caravan route. I thought this very probable, and from then on it seemed to me not at all impossible that it was the Romans who built Abalessa fort, whose architecture, undoubtedly, is of its sort quite unique in the central Sahara and bears no likeness at all to the easily recognizable Berber or 'Arab' ruins.

However, I was to make, in the course of my investigations, a discovery that was still more extraordinary. Pliny, in fact, mentions that Cornelius Balbus reached several rivers, one of which bore the name of 'Dasibari'. Various texts which have come down to us from the Greek and Latin authors tell us that the Sahara, at the time Pliny wrote, had already taken on a notably desert character. The *wadis*, as we call them now, no longer ran water save on occasion, that is to say they were already dried-up watercourses and not rivers at all. All the same, the desert character must have been less marked than today since horses could still be driven over the Sahara, though many precautions had to be taken, and the Libyans when travelling had to sling water-skins under the bellies of their mounts.

Where, then, can we possibly place the rivers Cornelius Balbus was said to have reached? To the south of Abalessa, that is to say, in the Hoggar? Had he, then, with Libyans as guides, followed the chariot route? That, indeed, is what he seemed to have done farther north, and if his aim was to traverse all the country of the Garamantes and to reconnoitre the main caravan route, it is obvious that he had to look for it farther south. But I could not think of any valley, right to the south of the Hoggar, any valley at all which might in Roman times have carried a great river.

I pored over my maps again, though I must say that I knew the country so well I could have done without them. All I could find was the valley of the Tilemsi, running south from the Adrar of the Iforas. But, well, I could not see any sort of resemblance between 'Tilemsi' and 'Dasibari'! There remained, then, the Niger itself. At first, it did seem rather improbable that Cornelius Balbus could have reached this mighty stream.

I had begun my deciphering at eight o'clock in the evening. My first identifications made me like a cat on hot bricks.

I felt sure I had got hold of a thread that was going to let me unravel a particularly tangled skein. At midnight I turned in, but I could not sleep a wink. The names in Pliny's text kept running through my head. So, at last, I lighted my lamp again. I went to look up a reference in one of my books and then got back to work. Suddenly—and it must have been very late in the night—I remembered that the Niger is called by the riverside populations the Songhoi, 'Isabari' from *isa* (river) and *bari* (big); in other words, the 'Great Stream'.

A comparison with 'Dasibari' seemed justified. But the text of Pliny may have suffered alteration, the name itself may have been incorrectly transcribed (such cases are frequent). Could the problem be considered as really solved? I searched again and turned over page after page of the old Songhoi dictionary which I had consulted so often in days gone by, when I had lived among the Niger fishermen between Timbuktu and Gao.

Then I remembered a detail of Songhoi folklore. According to traditions still lively among the river-dwellers, the masters of the stream were the Das, who are still called in those parts 'the lords of the river' or 'the lords of the water'. To this day the Niger is sometimes designated as *Da Isa Bari*, that is, 'The Great River of the Das'. So, 'Dasibari' may possibly have been a contraction of 'Da Isa Bari'. If this was the case, then the Niger really was the river referred to by Pliny and, despite all accepted ideas, the Romans in A.D. 19 may have crossed the Sahara from north to south and reached the great river of the Sudan.

It was six o'clock in the morning and dawn was breaking when, quite tired out, I slumped down on my bed. I had the feeling that I had been engaged in an epic battle.

When I woke up I was inclined to think that I had been the victim of a nightmare. Still, my maps were scattered over the floor, my pencilled notes, underscored in blue and red, lay on the shelf that I used as a bedside table . . . and all this proved to me that I had not just been dreaming.

So the poor little engravings and paintings on the rocks, pictures made by unknown men in the Tassili and the Hoggar and the Adrar of the Iforas and in other places, drawings executed maybe in idle moments, had revealed a secret which had quite baffled many scholars for many years.

I must hasten to admit that, of course, not everyone is convinced by my deductions. Some of my identifications have been readily admitted, indeed they can hardly be doubted, but others have been questioned. It is evident that a fine inscription relating to the *III Legio Augusta* in the Hoggar, or the Adrar, or better still, a Roman skeleton complete with armour (such as I have been challenged to produce!), would be pretty conclusive evidence. However, unfortunately, despite all my searching, neither the one nor the other has turned up—yet. But that does not mean that we shall never find such things in the future. Indeed, one fine day I did discover in a shelter at Sefar a slab of limestone bearing the words in red ochre III LEGIO AUGUSTA ITER PRAETER CAPUT SAXI, but its author was not far off. Michel Brézillon had been just killing time.

Up to now archaeological research in the immensity of the Sahara has been rather extensive than intensive. New means of transport will, in a few years, supplant the archaic camel (whose past services, however, are too often underestimated), and will allow explorers and researchers to make prolonged sojourns in regions now so difficult of access. The methodical excavation of the thousands of prehistoric tombs that dot the desert from the Atlas foothills to the Niger's banks will become possible and many new and surprising things will be revealed to us.

13

A Dying People:
The Tuareg of the Tassili

JEBRIN got more and more fidgety and was for ever finding excuses for leaving the camp. He had, as a matter of fact, less and less work, for we had settled down at Sefar for a good many weeks. Since all the massif had been explored he had practically nothing more to do except to look after the few donkeys we had nearby and see that they would be there if we needed them. I could not ask him to maintain communications with Djanet for he was certainly too old for such a task; in fact, each time he found it a little more difficult to clamber up the passes. If he stayed with us at all that was because he was fed regularly and got wages, that were by no means to be despised. It is rare enough for any Tuareg to be so lucky as to get a salary paid him for as long as fourteen months. All the same, Jebrin was intolerant of restraint and prized his complete liberty above anything else. So time began to weigh on his hands. The long wait seemed to him very boring indeed, and he was all the more impatient since his savings, which might have amounted to a quite respectable sum, had surely melted away. The Tuareg, who have been accustomed for ages to living from day to day, just cannot save money. As soon as they have any they cannot resist the temptation of the Djanet shops. The Tuareg will start off with something for himself, prob-

134

ably some of the stuff known as 'Malta cotton' dyed a deep indigo blue and having a very shiny surface. This cloth he gives to his wife so that she may make him an ample *gandurah* and a *sarual* in which he will strut about among his fellows.[1]

Whether they are rich or poor the Tuareg are much given to what may be called vestimentary display. Both men and women are very fond of scent and especially of Bulgarian Attar of Roses, with which they drench themselves so that the air around them becomes sickening to breathe. Then the women help to empty the men's pockets, for the ladies are even more coquettish than the men, and very greedy, they love shiny *gandurahs*, violently coloured artificial silk shawls with long fringes which come from the Lyons looms and are worked with a representation of the Mosque at Mecca. In the eyes of the Tuareg this holy picture confers talismanic virtues on the stuffs it adorns.

Among all the Tassili Tuareg no one, during the last thirty years, has derived more profit from the presence of the French in the Sahara than Jebrin. He is considered, and rightly so, as the best guide in the whole region. All the military reconnaissances, all the expeditions which for various reasons have made prospections on the plateau, all the tourists who have sought solitude and fantastically beautiful scenery have been conducted by Jebrin. Because he had been the guide of our French camel-corps detachments a price was put on his head by the Italians when they were still the lords of Ghat. But the old fellow was far too cunning to fall into their clutches.

Nevertheless, extraordinary as it may seem, although Jebrin has made a good deal of money during his career, he is still poor today. The main reason for this state of things is that all the men of the Kel Medak, his tribe, have taken advantage of him. When he brought back with him tea, sugar, flour, dates and stuffs, then, of

[1] A *gandurah* is the long robe the Tuareg wear and a *sarual* is trousers.

course, he was invited to each encampment. In fact he was throughout the Tassili regarded as the most profitable member of his tribe. Thus he enjoyed great prestige in all the camps, and this high reputation explains, in part at least, why Jebrin was able to escape so easily from the Italian agents who strove in vain to lure him into a trap at Ghat.

But much of his good luck was due to his own cunning. Jebrin is, in fact, an old fox and you must always play with him a game as astute as his own. Although I was certain that I could count on him in an emergency, nevertheless I had to put up a resistance, all the time, against his encroachments, I would even say against his exactions, for he was very greedy of gain and any means (he was never at a loss to find some new trick) were good if he thought they would serve his ends. Often I let him go ahead, but I was never fooled by him. I knew the Tuareg mentality of old, but then I could never overlook the excellent services (well paid, of course) he had rendered to our camel-corps detachments and, indeed, to our own expedition.

This side of the Tuareg character is well known to all who have lived among the people. Whether they be of noble race or of servile origin, they all behave with a familiarity and a lack of constraint which generally ends by estranging even those who are most disposed to like the Veiled Men. They are for ever begging for something and never leave one a minute's peace. As soon as you meet them they demand tea and sugar and often the shirt off your back. If you do not know how to deal with them you run a good chance of being stripped as naked as the day you were born; in fact that sort of experience has literally been the lot of some travellers. Of course, one must not expect to meet with the slightest gratitude—it would be puerile to expect it. At Aouanrhet, for instance, where we had been encamped for several weeks, there came up to us one day three Kel Medak Tuareg, who had learned

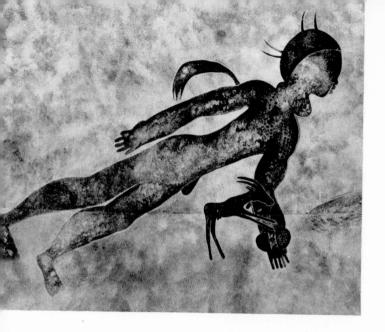

43. Ti-n-Tazarift: The Swimmer: 'Round Heads' Period: (Evolved)

44. Ti-n-Tazarift: The Archer: 'Round Heads' Period: (Evolved)

45. Ti-n-Tazarift: Recumbent Woman: 'Round Heads' Period: (Decadent)

46. Ti-n-Tazarift: Schematic Cattle: Bovidian Period

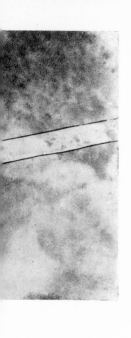

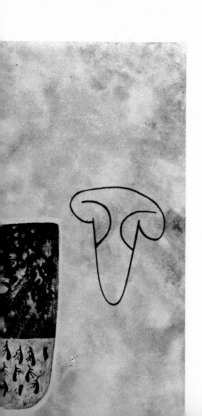

47. Ti-n-Tazarift: The
Negro Dancer with
bound legs: Pre-Bovidian
but undetermined period

48. Ti-n-Tazarift: The Dancers: Post-Bovidian Period with Egyptian Influence

49. Ti-n-Tazarift: Hippopotamuses: Bovidian Period

of our presence in that isolated spot and had made a detour of more than five miles to visit us. In customary manner they came forward to salute me and to greet us. Then they settled themselves down near the cookhouse where our boy Mohammed was preparing a meal. So, at luncheon-time they shared the contents of our saucepans and drank tea with us. Then, as our stock of wood was very low, I asked one of the Tuareg to go and fetch some faggots from a neighbouring *wadi*.

'If you give me money I go, if not I will not go,' was the reply.

So he stayed stretched out on the sand with his two friends, but that evening the trio were all ready for dinner. So, to give them a good lesson, I pretended we had had no wood, and had cooked nothing for them. They were much annoyed, rose up, and with great dignity disappeared without a word of farewell. This sort of behaviour is common enough among the Tuareg, who do not feel—apart from the strictly conventional rules of hospitality— any sort of social obligation at all. 'Nothing for nothing'—at any rate as far as Europeans are concerned—is the Tuareg rule of life. All their actions are dictated by the hope or expectation of benefits to be extorted from us. As some excuse for their behaviour— although not a complete exoneration—we must admit that their means of existence, in a desert land, are very scanty. Indeed, they have to struggle, without a moment's respite, against their environment. Perhaps we might compare the Tuareg with wolves, and the laws of the Sahara are as implacable as those of the forest or the jungle. In fact, the Tuareg would behave with each other as they do with us did not the very conditions of their lives make some mutual aid an absolute necessity.

The Tassili Tuareg number about three thousand five hundred, and they are scattered about over an area almost as large as that of France;[1] they are, moreover, the most wretchedly poor of all the

[1] That is, about 213,000 square miles.

Tuareg. Never in the course of my journeyings among the tribes of the Hoggar or the Sudan have I met with so much misery of every sort. Rare indeed are the Tassili families which possess a good tent— whereas in the Hoggar it is a point of honour to have a fine covering made of mouflon skins, carefully sewn together and adorned with little tassels which themselves are ornamented with guilloches and open-work designs, often in excellent, though sober, taste. But the tents of the Ker Ajjer people are all holes and patches, while the 'veil' which, according to tradition, must shelter each newly married couple, is absurdly small and made of poorly tanned skins. The fact is that, first and foremost, the Tassili people are troglodytes, which is not surprising, in view of the geological formation of their country and of the existence of innumerable natural shelters hollowed out of the sandstone. By living in caves the Tassili Tuareg are but following the tradition of their pre-historic forerunners and especially of the neolithic pastoralists who not only had straw huts (to be seen in several of the paintings) but also used the rock-shelters as kitchens and as stables for their animals. We came across several families settled in such age-old dens and protected by two low walls of stone. It was hard to tell whether the walls had been set up recently or if they dated from the time of the 'Bovidians'. When we asked them we were told that the walls had 'always been there', but that, in some cases, they would set up a new wind-break, easy enough to build since stones abound on every side. Why did they do this? Well, certain shelters had the reputation of being haunted by *jinnūn*.

Like all Tuareg, Jebrin was extremely superstitious. He had a firm belief in ghosts and from time to time I would come across him burning, on the hot ashes, the seeds of a small plant that gave off a particularly revolting odour, which, however, was calculated to chase away very quickly any evil spirits which might be lingering about. He explained this with perfect seriousness and moreover practically admitted that he himself had seen, or heard, the demons.

The rudimentary shelters offer, nonetheless, a fairly good protection against both the harsh winters and the scorching summers (we were ourselves able to verify this during our sixteen months' stay), but the Tuareg furniture is reduced to a strict minimum . . . one or two earthenware pots, sometimes an enamelled vessel—bought in a shop—one or two wooden bowls botched up with bits of wire, a mortar and a wooden pestle out of shape from long use, two or three old spoons, a kettle, two enamelled tea-pots filthy with soot, a little wooden bucket cut out of tamaris wood (and used in milking the goats), a funnel of the same wood, well coated with dirt, one or two water-skins and a small skin for churning . . . that comprises about all the worldly goods of a married couple. The prevailing poverty is such that no one takes any notice of the battered and antique appearance of the utensils.

The Tassili Tuareg women seem to be less industrious than those in other areas, and although a little working of hides and skins is done, the tanning is so poor that the saddle-sacks (which among the Tuareg of the Hoggar and the Adrar of the Iforas are often of high quality and even of artistic value) are very indifferent. During all the course of my various visits to the Tassili I rarely, if ever, saw decently made saddle-bags.

Again, in the Hoggar every woman can, in a few hours and with the help of some bits of skin, make a comfortable pair of sandals; the Tassili women seem, however, to have lost the knack—if they ever had it—so that everyone goes about barefoot, in winter as well as in summer, and that is a very uncomfortable way of walking in a land that is all rocks and stones. All the same, if the Tassili women cared to give themselves the trouble they could earn a good deal of money by making sandals.

As it is, the only income of the Kel Ajjer comes from their
flocks and from a few loads of wood they sell at Djanet . . . the
whole does not amount to much, especially if we think that a
family just manages, in a good year, to sell about twenty goats, a
few pounds of butter, some water-skins, approximately twenty
loads of wood . . . the whole lot worth from seventy to eighty
thousand francs,[1] and that must suffice a family numbering, with
the children, five or six persons, for a whole year.

Since they have not enough camels, the Kel Ajjer practically
never organize caravans to the Sudan and do not (as do the Kel
Hoggar) take any part in the working of the Amadror salt deposits.

Undernourishment is, then, general. Many families have to
make do with one meal a day and it is composed of either a date
'stew' or of a *tajela*,[2] to which is added a little curdled buttermilk
and one or two spoonfuls of butter.

When they are old enough to tend the goats the children have
to fend for themselves as best they can. They hunt lizards and
little rodents called *gundi*, and are remarkably clever at catching
these creatures. A lizard or a *gundi* is as good as a beefsteak for one
of the urchins, but you may often see them in winter come home
with empty hands—and stomachs—since none of the beasts had
ventured out of its hole. Then the children would crowd round
us at meal-times and scrape away hungrily at the bottom of
our pots and pans. The grown-up people also do not, of course,
despise such little pickings, though if there were children in the
camp the adults gave way to them, for they knew well enough that
young stomachs felt more keenly the need for food. These Tassili
Tuareg, moreover, seem to have stomachs like those of camels,
that is to say, capable of digesting all sorts of queer plants—especially
the false asparagus of the sands (very bitter this), the seeds of the

[1] Worth, maybe (in 1958), £60 to £70 or $180 to $200.
[2] A sort of cake made of ground wheat, without yeast, and cooked in the hot ashes.
(Author's note.)

tulult and the *merokba*, the berries of the *Spina Christi* and the leaves
of the wild sorrel. On the day that a hare is caught in a trap there
is general rejoicing, the *baraka*, or blessing of God, has been mani-
fested. Some of the most skilful hunters manage, from time to
time, to kill a mouflon or a gazelle, but that happens very seldom.

Undernourishment, naturally enough, induces rickets, although
most of the Tassili Tuareg are of vigorous appearance and of
remarkable endurance on the march. It is only fair to add that
natural selection operates pretty drastically since the infantile
mortality rate is about 50 per cent. Jebrin had had twelve children
by two wives; only six of his offspring were alive at the time we
were in the Tassili and one, at least, of his surviving sons was
certainly not destined to make old bones. The children grow up
without any sort of attention. As they live among their herds many
of them amuse themselves by sucking goat droppings and smearing
themselves with goat's urine—the mothers never seem to think
of preventing such things. The boys' and girls' eyes are covered
with flies and are always running, so that conjunctivitis, ophthalmia
and trachoma are common and leave traces that mark the children
for the rest of their lives. Physical deformities are common. We
noticed a certain number of club-feet and other congenital mal-
formations of both feet and hands. There are many cases of strabis-
mus and alveolar abnormalities are very usual. They are probably
induced by avitaminosis and calcium deficiency.

It is in winter that the results of under-feeding are most marked
and severe, and at that time of year it is rare to come across an
encampment where there is not someone sick. The nomads,
indeed, are ill protected from the cold, they have no woollen
clothes and only thin, cotton garments. All, therefore, complain
of what they call the 'chill in their bones', that is to say, of articular
rheumatism. The winter is the season the Tassili Tuareg fear the
most for the climate is pitiless and kills off the weaker. During the

cold weather we spent among these people one of Jebrin's wives and his aunt died within a few weeks of each other. Jebrin himself and Matal, one of his sons (a wretchedly skinny lad of about sixteen), also nearly died. Many deaths were reported from the encampments near us. However, nothing would induce the Tassili men to go down to Djanet and take advantage of the really magnificent infirmary which had just been built specially for them. Like the mouflon, they would rather die among their native rocks. If Jebrin, indeed, did consent, from time to time, to go and be treated at the infirmary, that was, no doubt, because he was one of the most sophisticated inhabitants of the Tassili, though, from many points of view, he was backward and old-fashioned.

One day when he got back to his encampment he found that one of his sons had just been bitten by a viper and was in rather bad shape, but instead of coming to our camp to get some serum (which he knew well enough existed since I had often given him elaborate explanations about it), Jebrin preferred to apply the traditional treatment, that is to say, he made a cut in the affected place and let it bleed. Such a method is very haphazard and un-reliable, especially if the bite is deep and a good deal of venom has been injected. So, of course, the boy's condition got worse and worse until, luckily enough, a subaltern commanding a camel-corps detachment at Djanet happened to pass by and was able to take measures just in time.

The fact was that Jebrin believed much more in the efficacy of jam than serum, and this belief was the result of a personal experience of his. Some years before, he had been bitten by a viper and for three months hovered between life and death. As soon as he felt well enough to undertake the journey, Jebrin went down to Djanet. The doctor who examined him noticed that the foot wound had healed up, but as a sort of reward for having had such a narrow escape, gave Jebrin a pot of jam. He did not understand that this was just a friendly gesture, but thought the jam was medicine and soon swallowed the whole pot. As he felt much better after this, our Jebrin ever afterwards swore that it was the dose of jam that banished his pains for good.

Regarding schools, Tuareg prejudices are about the same as those concerning hospitals. The Tassili men will not send their children to school at Djanet, although the government authorities are quite prepared to pay for board and lodging.

'No,' Jebrin would say, 'we are not made to live in mud huts and learn to count like tradesmen. We, the Tuareg of the Tassili, are made to live among our rocks and with our goats and camels—nothing else. That's the life we like. It's the life our fathers and our grandfathers led. We know that we are no longer of any account, but we are not like the Kel Djanet, we will not send our children to school.'

The Kel Djanet. That is, the inhabitants of the oasis, the people who tend palm-trees, till the soil, send their children to school, get jobs as workmen, serve as cooks and house-boys in French families, and so forth, for such people the Tuareg feel nothing but the greatest contempt, though they admit that the standard of living is much higher in the oases than on their plateau.

In such circumstances, we may well ask what, in the near future, will happen to the Tassili Tuareg. They are determined to stay among their rocks, they are obstinately opposed to all social change, they are in poor shape physiologically through under-nourishment, they are tainted by too many consanguineous marriages, so they seem destined to disappear in a relatively short time. Of course, it may be objected that a similar prophecy was made about fifty years ago with regard to the Hoggar Tuareg and that, all the same, today these tribesmen are getting on very well indeed. They have even doubled in numbers, but then, their living

conditions have also been very definitely bettered, whereas their
brethren of the Tassili have just been able to keep up their numbers and their condition has been, at no time, ameliorated. Can,
then, anything be done about the Tassili Tuareg? Their whole
problem boils itself down to this—increase in agricultural resources. Only such increase could give new vitality to a human
group now in decadence, though in the past it was once flourishing
enough.

For we should not forget that at one time the Tassili Tuareg
played a considerable role in history. During centuries they were
the undisputed masters of the Fezzan. Their chieftains ruled over
the Hoggar and controlled the great caravan highway from Tripoli
in the north to the Sudan in the south. Their capital, Garama,
gave its name to all the men of their stock, the ancient Garamantes; their fame crossed the Mediterranean and they took part,
with our ancestors of the Gaulish contingents, in the battles of
Trebiae, of Cannae and of the Trasimene Lake. Hannibal's army,
indeed, included a large cavalry corps of Tuareg. Their decline
dates from the Moslem invasions which drove them out of the
Fezzan. Rather than accept the new masters and adopt the faith
of Islam the Tuareg preferred to take refuge among the Tassili
rocks whither the Moslem conquerors never dared to follow
them. However, once the Tuareg reached their new home, their
numbers caused a famine, while dissensions broke out among the
tribes, many of which were obliged to seek their fortune in richer
and less populated areas. A good many of the Tuareg settled in the
Air, where they remained until, under pressure from newcomers,
also driven south, the Air Tuareg must set out on a search for
other lands. The vanguard of the emigration pushed as far as the
Lake Chad region, where its descendants, mingled and intermixed
with Negroes, present but faint traces of their Tuareg origin.
From the period of the Islamic invasions, then, the Tassili acted

as a sieve that drained off the surplus population which it could not nourish.

Later on, but before the French pacified the region, the Saharan Tuareg, those of the Hoggar and the Ajjer, lived as bandits and preyed on the people of the oases, while the traffic in slaves captured in the Sudan allowed the Tuareg to maintain themselves as a flourishing community. They went abroad, with weapons in their hands, and sought far from home what their own country refused them. But such times are long past and it must be hoped that they will never come back. Still, the tragedy of the Tassili Tuareg is with us, since these men, if left to the scanty resources of their stony plateau, can do nothing but just keep alive, and that miserably enough.

Something, then, must be done to increase the local resources, and since Tuareg life today depends almost entirely upon stock-raising, the whole problem is really one of pasturage. And pastures mean water. The Tassili should once again be green with vegetation as it was when it supported elephant, rhinoceros, giraffe and herds of cattle. Is such a thing possible? Yes, when the scientists can produce artificial rain as and when needed, but, alas, they cannot do this yet, despite all that has been written on the subject of rain-making. As far as I can see, however, rain would afford the only possible solution to the Tuareg problem, for I do not think that the men of the Tassili will ever move off to the Edjelé oil-fields.

If they cannot get rain, then I think we shall have to resign ourselves to seeing the disappearance of the Veiled Men of the Tassili, those proud highwaymen, those somehow attractive brigands who for centuries ruled the Sahara and whose very name sufficed to paralyse with terror the poor Negroes of the Sudan and the oases and even the neighbouring 'Arabs', whose great enemies the Tuareg once were.

K

14

The Fresco of Twelve Phases

ORK progressed at Sefar. Michel Brézillon and André Vila kept at it from morning to night and the quality of their copies had become absolutely irreproachable. With Michel we tackled an astounding fresco which was to prove the most complex of all those we had seen. It was situated in a low-roofed shelter with a floor thickly covered in sand. The painting itself was some fifty feet long, and when we came to examine it closely we discovered that it comprised no less than twelve different layers of paintings which related to as many archaeological phases all of which preceded the 'Bovidian' epoch. The layers, then, were very ancient. With the help of Lajoux it took me a week to make the tracings, but when it came to colouring the copy then our problem was baffling, a tracing indeed just secures that the figures should be in their right places. But many of the figures had been partially obliterated by others while not a few had been seriously damaged. All this made our work extremely ticklish. We were faced, in fact, with a unique example (I think that the Abbé Breuil will bear me out in this) of prehistoric rupestral art, since never before had an archaeologist had the opportunity of viewing so many over-paintings representing so many different art-phases, indeed such a jumble and tangle. Sometimes Michel and I differed in our views. He would have it that such and such a layer came over another, while I was just as sure that the opposite was true.

To revive the colours we sprinkled the wall with water and we tried to find which was the best lighting. The fact was that light striking the surface from the right would bring out well enough a red or yellow ochre, while light coming from the left would make the whites and greenish tones stand out. The result was that we had to go back, ten times a day, to one single spot. Finally, however, our very careful examination did allow us to come to an agreement. The whole task was not only sometimes confusing, but it was always very fatiguing. We had to take up positions that were very often highly uncomfortable. Still, we did not mind; we were, all the time, finding out more and more about each of the art-styles so that, later on, we were able to solve some problems of considerable archaeological importance. Our system of copying the colours on the spot, though it forced us to worry out the whole assemblage piecemeal, can be rivalled by no other technique whether that of diagrammatic tracing or photography (even if we take into account the employment of infra-red lighting); these methods are useful as affording additional checking but are not of themselves alone sufficient.

In this shelter, once again, we found little figures in violaceous ochre which seemed to belong to the most ancient art-phase. What dominated everything were representations of white mouflon outlined in red. They were marching in procession along the whole length of the picture. But there were also elephants, a giraffe, antelopes, *Hippotraginae* (i.e. such creatures as sable and roan ante-lopes, oryx and addax), and yet other mouflon belonging to another art-phase and painted in yellow ochre with red outlines. These animals were marked by the long hair of their legs and necks. The figures belonged to the same artistic group as the human representations with round heads of the 'Martian' type (two specimens of which appear on this fresco) and are executed in the same pigments. There were also over-painted human figures in white with delicate and elongated limbs. One of these

pictures annoyed Michel, who accused me of copying 'immoral'
scenes. If, however, the ancient Tassilians anticipated Rabelais,
that was not my fault. Lastly, above the mass of paintings, was a
military scene representing individuals armed with bows and
belonging, apparently, to the art-phase of the herdsmen.

To my great astonishment I discovered that these warriors were
not men but women, and that, moreover, each one of them displayed only one breast. Women archers we had not, up to that
time, encountered, and they went to enrich our documents
concerning the astonishing 'Bovidian' people. Was this single
breast just an artistic convention or an appearance suggested by
the drawing or did the models suffer an ablation of one of their
breasts? One is reminded of the amazons of King Behanzin (of
Dahomey), those bloody women who composed the bodyguard
of the black monarch and cut off their right breasts so as not to be
hampered in their military exercises. Did the Tassili pastoralists
also have amazons?

The 'Little Mouflon' fresco (since that is the name we gave it
finally) afforded us much precious evidence since thanks to it we
were able to construct a relative chronology covering this epoch
of the twelve art-phases, and this data, added to the observations
we had already made, allowed us to get a more exact idea of the
evolution of Tassili prehistoric art.

I use the word 'art', for what our chronology represents on the
human scale is quite another matter. We saw clearly enough that
the styles varied, but nothing allows us to conclude that such
variations corresponded, in every case, with differences of an
ethnical sort, or still less that such and such an art-phase can be
equated with any given human group. All one can advance is
this: the Sahara seems to have been inhabited, before the arrival
of the cattle-breeding pastoralists, by negroid populations. The
fauna does not present, from one phase to the other, any notable

difference which could be interpreted as indicating a change of climate. Indeed, the representations of animals seem to indicate that the fauna was for long stable in the sense that the same species are represented both in the most ancient art-phases and in those of the 'Bovidian' period. It is not until the 'Equine Period' (marked by the appearance of horse-drawn chariots) that any marked change is to be seen; then the larger mammals (such as hippopotamus, rhinoceros and elephant) disappear, though the giraffe, antelope and ostrich remain. Therefore the desiccation of the Sahara must have begun between the fourth and second millennia B.C. Of course, we must bear in mind, too, that the 'bestiary' of the Tassili painters did not, necessarily, offer a complete list of the animals existing in the desert at any given period.

Another shelter that we baptized the 'Big Circus' provided also most interesting information about the evolution of art-styles. The over-paintings at this site comprise, mostly, human figures with round heads. This style seems, during the course of ages, to have been subjected to a number of variations, so it was important to distinguish between the various techniques. Here, again, the work was most fatiguing and tricky. Some pictures were more than twelve feet above the level of the ground, and we had to perform acrobatic feats in order to reach them. Our folding iron ladder had been knocked about for months and had had to be held together with bits of string so that it wobbled most alarmingly under our weight when we struggled against the wind that blew the sheets of paper about and raised whirlwinds of sand around us. We had to find other means and piled our tables one on top of the other. At last, after hours of effort, with one of us holding up the other, we did manage to make a copy of the whole assemblage (more than ten yards square) with the exception of some figures too high up and too effaced for us to draw them. This experience strengthened our conviction that the prehistoric artists must have used some sort of scaffolding to execute paintings so high up on the rock-face, since the level of the ground does not seem to have changed since the times of the ancient dwellers on the Tassili.

All this work, we hoped, at least, would find its reward some time or another, but for the time being we had to be satisfied with the eternal dish of noodles that awaited us at midday and in the evening. It was not very comforting fare. Then, again, our complete isolation sometimes got us down.

Still, we were not quite forgotten in our rocky refuge for every Sunday the mail-plane from Algiers flew over us. We knew the crews for we had met them either at the Djanet mess or we had flown with them. They knew where we were and dipped wings in salute each time they came across while we waved back from our camp.

One day, quite suddenly, the plane swooped down on us in a roar like thunder. Indeed the machine flew so low that its noise reverberated through our caverns and almost split our ears. This was not at all the sort of thing our friendly pilots would be likely to do.

Lajoux, who happened to be on a neighbouring spur of rock in order to take a panoramic view, raised his arms instinctively to salute the intruder. A little disconcerted, he came and rejoined us and we all laughed at the pilot's little joke.

However, two days later my old guide Sermi and another Tuareg arrived at our camp. They were absolutely exhausted. Sermi held out to me an envelope on which I recognized the writing of my friend Rossi, the officer commanding the Djanet post:

My dear Lhote,
    The pilot of the DC3 which has just landed at Djanet tells me that he noticed on the Tassili a European who was waving

his arms about desperately and apparently calling for help. I at once sent off to you two *goumiers* with orders to find you as soon as possible. If the signals meant something then send Sermi back to me in all haste. If your man was just waving good day to the fliers then please tell your young men not to indulge in such playful pranks in the future.

Yours ever, R.

I read the letter aloud to all our party and saw from their expressions that they had expected some serious news when they had seen two *goumiers* armed to the teeth. I had hardly finished speaking when apprehension was drowned in general hilarity.

Poor Sermi and his companion had marched day and night for forty-eight hours since they did not know just where our camp was. First of all they went to Jabbaren, then on to Ti-n-Bedjadj, and from there to Tamrit where they picked up our tracks left on the sands a month before. The Tuareg, indeed, are marvellous sleuths and their ability to read imprints on the ground says much for their keen powers of observation.

During the forty-eight hours of their search they had eaten nothing for they had met no one. So, like ourselves, they had a good right to a dish of noodles, and to as many helpings as they could manage plus as much tea as they could drink.

I wrote back to Rossi that all was well; I thanked him warmly for his kindness. This little incident cheered us up a good deal, since it proved that we had friends on whom we could really count in case of emergency.

Sefar was to reveal other marvels to us. First of all, there was a huge human figure hardly visible so pale was its colouring and so effaced were some parts of it. It wore a helmet surmounted by a crest for all the world like that of the ancient Greeks' military head-dress. The figure was of the same type as the 'Antinea' of Jabbaren, the same slate-grey tone, the same head-dress with a white outline and enlivened with red bands. It was a painting of exceptionally high quality and it presented, as did so many other of the same school, a very puzzling enigma indeed. On the opposite bank of the *wadi* another painting represented a large Negress wearing a mask over her face. The figure belonged to the same art-phase as that of the Round-Heads, but this picture was in an 'evolved' style. Many little 'Bovidian' figures were on the same rock-wall. They presented no problem, but the scenes in which they took part were astoundingly life-like and realistic. There was an extraordinary combat of archers, vigorous and lively and con-veying the emotions that animated the opposing parties.

Still another discovery, among the hundreds we made, deserves a mention. Lajoux and I examined carefully all the walls of the shelters. As he had more time at his disposal than his comrades, our film-man did the preliminary prospecting and then if he reported something interesting we all went together to inspect what he had found. One day we had explored a series of shelters and were just getting ready to go back to the camp when I made out through a hole in the rock something that looked like a dark recess.

'Did you have a look at that?'

'No, it didn't seem a likely place for pictures.'

'Let's go and see, all the same.'

The shelter, which was rather overhung, was long and might well have served as a dwelling-place. We searched the walls and made out a long red line broken in three places. Generally speak-ing I could nearly always make out from certain signs what art-phase and what sort of subject I was dealing with, even if the painting was very effaced or obliterated by a coating of

50. Sefar. The Great God with Suppliant Women.
Decadent Period of 'Round Heads' Photograph of the rock-wall

51. Sefar: 'Greek Warrior': Post-Bovidian Period with Egyptian Influence

52. *Sefar: Detail of Central Mask: Post-Bovidian Period with Egyptian Influence. (Photograph of the Rock-Face)*

53. *Sefar: Stylized Negro Masks: Post-Bovidian Period with Egyptian Influence*

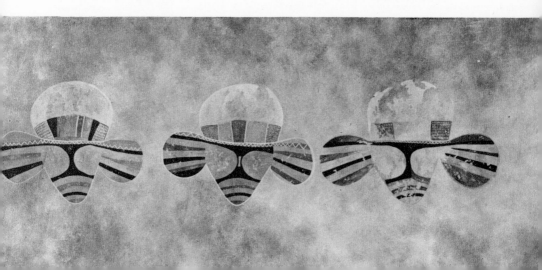

54. *Sefar: 'Negatives' of Hands: Post-Bovidian Period. (Photograph of the Rock-Face)*

55. *Sefar: The Shelter of the Child*ren: Bovidian Period

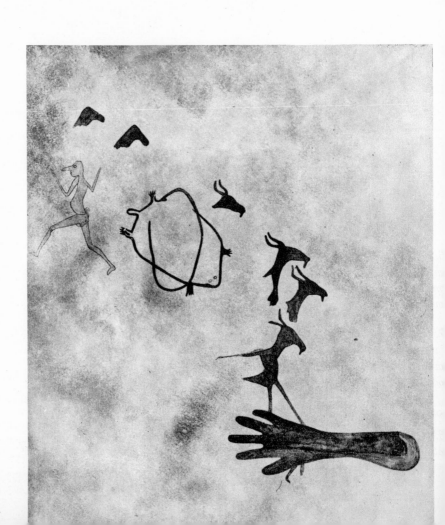

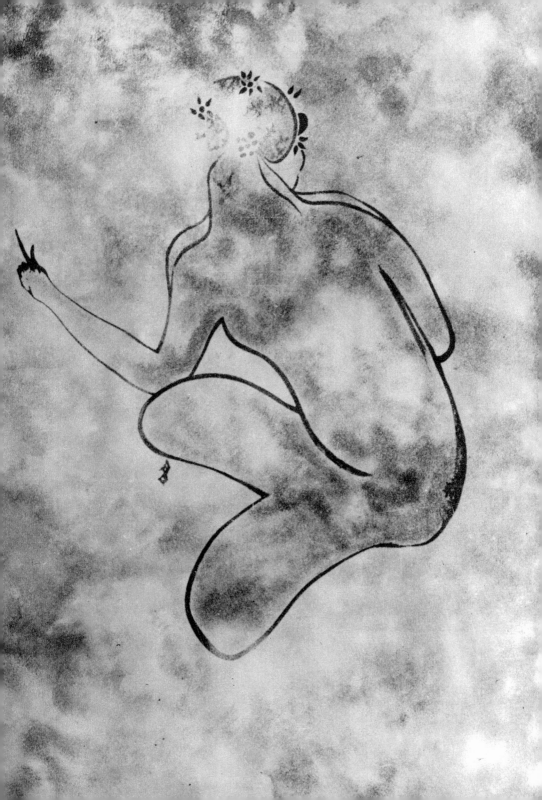

59. *Sefar: Men with Tridents: 'Round Heads' Period: (Ancient)*

60. *Sefar: Masked Men and Women Dancing: 'Round Heads' Period: (Evolved and with Egyptian Influence)*

clayey dust. But this time the lines I saw conveyed nothing to me and I could make out no details at all.

'Bah,' said Lajoux, 'just a few scribblings of no interest.'

We had no more water and the pool was rather far off. All the same, I said to Lajoux, 'Go and get some water, just on the off-chance; it may be worth while, and if there's nothing, why, our minds will be at rest.'

We took our little water-skin and dashed some water against the wall; no sooner had the trickles made their way down the rock than we uttered cries of admiration. Swabbing, once more, re-vealed things hidden, for there were three Negro masks, very stylized and placed side by side on the same level. They looked just like the motifs in some ultra-modern scheme of decoration. The noses and mouths were curiously schematized and the faces indicated by a simple oval outline. The whole thing measured over six feet long. After a very careful examination I noticed in the head-dresses several parallel strips of different colours but exactly similar to those in our crested figure, the same tones, slate-grey, red ochre, white outlines. Though there was no likeness between styles or subjects, still the identity of technique was undeniable.

So it would seem that there must have been, at one and the same epoch, artists who practised both naturalism and symbolism. These works of art appear to be the product of an amalgam be-tween Egyptian and Negro artistic traditions and may well in-dicate, also, ethnical coexistence; that is to say, the simultaneous presence of men who had been subjected on the one hand to Graeco-Egyptian and on the other hand to negroid influences. Such possibilities, in any case, indicate the great interest of the Tassili paintings for scientists and art-historians.

On our way back we were to find two other fine paintings. One of them represented a strange animal (that was more than a yard long) painted in yellow ochre with the outlines red and looking like a big triton, while the second was an enormous warthog showing all his teeth. It belonged apparently to the same art-phase as that of the 'Great God'.

The last observation we made on this outing was that all the exits of the valleys were barred with little stone walls so that we were, in fact, in a small fortified camp.

At Jabbaren and at Ouan Abou I had already noticed the same sort of thing, and I am inclined to think that these defensive works must be attributed to the 'Bovidian' people. Furthermore, at Sefar in the corridor we called 'The Negress' there were to be seen in the middle of the dip in the ground three foundations of ancient huts. The outlines were still easy to trace and their forms recalled those of the huts painted on the shelter-walls.

Different sorts of discoveries awaited us in camp. The first warm days were upon us. Vipers' traces and tracks could be seen on all sides. I killed the first snake at the foot of a wild olive-tree around which Lajoux and I were wandering in the hope of finding a flower, which no herbarium in the world yet contains. I found a second viper a few paces from our tents. The creature was, after a fruitful raid on our kitchen, coiled up in the shelter of a stone. I came across a third under a clump of *arta* while I was showing Michel the way to a pool which had just been discovered. In fact, there was a real invasion of serpents. Never, as yet, had we come across any area so infested with vipers as Sefar. It is true that the site is particularly favourable for the reptiles, since the Tuareg hardly ever camp there and, therefore, there is no one to interfere with the creatures.

Right at the beginning of his stay with us Lesage nearly got bitten. He put his foot down about four inches from the viper, but Vila, who had spotted the beast, yelled out to him, and he jumped back as white as a sheet. It took him some time to recover his wits, and for days afterwards he talked of nothing but his miraculous escape. The adventure was, it must be admitted, alarming enough. The snake was an enormous female with a head as large as a dollar piece, though in Lesage's vivid imagination the snake's proportions swelled up still more formidably. Under the influence of the fright and the realization that he had escaped by the skin of his teeth, Lesage made a vow to go and burn a candle at the shrine of Notre Dame de la Garde when he returned to Marseilles. It was to be a candle as long as the viper and certainly at the time he credited the reptile with a most respectable size.

When he got back to France, Lesage kept his word, but he maintained that the expedition ought to pay for the candle. However, Michel, who kept the accounts (and was only too aware of the size of our deficit, anyway), said, and we all approved, that it was not the expedition which had made the vow and could not, therefore, be held responsible for the cost of the candle. Nonetheless, we all went up to the sanctuary, though the length of the viper had by this time shrunk to that of a baby snake, and the candle, which was to have been no less than eleven feet long, was reduced to the modest height of a small taper.

During the summer our camp was transformed into a menagerie. Vila made a collection of *dobs*—large lizards with spiky tails, and so tame and harmless that the zoologists have baptized them *Uromastix acantherinus*. They were of all sizes, and Vila put bits of string round their bellies and, so that they could not escape, attached them to cords, quite near our messing space. Moreover, he managed to get them back alive to Paris. They are now in a showcase at the Vivarium in the *Jardin des Plantes*. There were also two leverets which we found at the foot of a bush of *drinn* in the Oued Sefar where their parents would come and gambol about under our eyes. We brought the little creatures up on powdered milk, but one of them died after a few days, though the other got very tame in a short time and soon was eating, without any tempting, the dandelions we brought him. Unfortunately he too died of heat-stroke when we got back to Djanet, for his box remained too long exposed to the sun.

Another boarder at our camp was a young *gundi* caught by the Tuareg children. This also became very tame. All these animals got on well enough together, like the creatures in Noah's Ark, though we would have rather liked a Flood.

15

Parachutes

A S TIME wore on the supply problem got more and more acute. Some of our provisions had run out. We had very little sugar left and our flour-sacks were three-quarters empty. Each time I asked Jebrin for camels or asses, he mumbled under his *litham*;[1] the upshot was that there was no encampment anywhere near us and furthermore, all the camels, by this time of year, had gone down to pasture in the Admer *erg*. To make matters worse, Captain Rossi at Djanet found it impossible to get me any pack-animals. It looked as though we were going to have to throw up the job.

As a last resort I called Jebrin and showed him the flabby flour-sacks. I asked him if he liked eating bricks because he would soon have to start on them.

'No, I've seen enough stones all my life and if you could eat them the Kel Medak would be a lot fatter than they are, for there's no lack of rocks in our country.'

Finally, Agaoued, our second *goumier*, turned up one morning with four donkeys and the little caravan set off post-haste for Djanet. Among the letters Agaoued brought back two days later I found a message. The parachute operation I had asked for several weeks earlier had been authorized and could start up as soon as I liked.

I at once got ready to go down to Djanet and resolved that on the way I would pick out the dropping area since there could be

[1] The Tuareg face-veil.

no question at all of releasing parachutes over the stone forest
where we were encamped. About three miles from camp, at the
junction of the Sefar and I-n-Itinen *wadis* I discovered a huge,
bare plateau. It was, indeed, a bit rocky and stony, but there was
no other choice, this was the only suitable place I could find.

When I got to Djanet there was bad news. The Junkers 52 whose
parachutist crew had volunteered for the operation had just
crashed at the end of the runway while taking off for a short
reconnaissance flight. Result, nine dead and two, who escaped by
a miracle, very badly wounded. The plane was smashed to
smithereens.

This catastrophe upset all our plans so I made up my mind to
go up to Algiers where, anyway, I was to meet Guichard on his
way back from France and organize with him a first showing of
our pictures.

In Algiers at the H.Q. of the Air Force we went into the possibilities of the parachuting operation. The resident Minister for
Algerian Affairs gave us his blessing, and I must say that everyone I
met was most helpful. There was, indeed, a general feeling of
interest in our mission, and ever since its difficult start had been
known we had met with nothing but kindness.

It was arranged that the Nord 2500 put at our disposal by the
Air Force authorities should, first of all, touch down at Fort-
Flatters where the oil-men were also awaiting supplies. Therefore
I sent off the painter Lesage (our new recruit) by the first mail-
plane to Djanet so that he could contact our expedition as soon as
possible. I gave Lesage detailed instructions for Brézillon whose
job was to be the co-ordinating of the ground operations. I reminded—or informed—Brézillon that he should pay particular
attention to the following six points:

1. The terrain I had chosen lay three miles south of our camp.
2. The terrain must be marked out at the corners (over an area

of five yards by five yards) with strips of drawing-paper held in place by stones. The marks must be in place three or four days before the actual date of the operation so that we could reconnoitre the terrain from the air on our flight to Djanet.

3. Smoke-fuses must be used (we had a small stock of them at the camp) at the appropriate time so as to indicate the direction of the wind on the ground.

4. Lajoux and Vila should arrange to film and photograph the operation—the first of its sort ever to be attempted in the mountains of the central Sahara.

5. As soon as the operation was over Lajoux should go down to Djanet so as to join me in taking air photographs the next day.

6. Arrangements should be made not only for transporting the supplies to our camp but also for the return of the empty containers and the parachutes to Djanet.

On 5th May at half past five in the morning at the Maison-Blanche airport in Algiers we met the crew who were to be so helpful in carrying out the operation: Captain Flachard, in command, Lieutenant Mothe, co-pilot, Sergeant Leblanc, navigator, Sergeant-Major Lassibille, radio operator, Warrant Officer Cabaret, engineer. In addition to this highly experienced team (several of whom had taken part in the Indo-China and Suez campaigns) there were Corporal Vasseur, a parachutist specialized in releasing containers, and young Charles Scherle, an Army photographer who had with him his camera for taking air photographs.

In the airport bar the atmosphere was that of the typical air force squadron, an atmosphere I had known so well years before, a few minutes of cheerful, easy friendliness, then a quick check-up and we took off for the south.

We touched down first at Ouargla where we put off some cargo and took on more. Then we stopped at Fort-Flatters where all the cargo was taken off and the mechanics filled up our petrol tanks.

We headed for Djanet. As soon as we neared the Tassili I took the co-pilot's seat so as to show the captain where he should go to make our preliminary reconnaissance of the terrain. But, as we were anxious not to get off our course or to waste time looking for our camp in the endless labyrinth of petrified forests, we pushed on to Djanet. When, however, we were over the oasis we headed for Sefar, taking a line I had drawn on the map; it was a rough indication of the route as given me by Jebrin on the ground.

This first flight, however, proved fruitless, and I began to wonder if our people really had put down the markings in place. Then I reflected that if they had not done this they would surely have lighted the smoke-fuses to indicate their whereabouts. We veered about and once more circled over Djanet, then we set off again, but this time we kept a little more towards the east. I soon spotted Tamrit and, from time to time, was able to make out the Djanet-Ghat track. Then we were over the forest of stones which must include the massifs of Tin Abou Teka, Ti-n-Tazarift and Sefar . . . still nothing to be seen. We swerved to the left . . . then Guichard, who had a better view than we had, for he was looking out of the rear porthole, saw the white strips of paper in their right places marking out the terrain very effectively. Soon we made out a large circle enclosing the word SEFAR . . . it was bang in the middle of our camp and was plainly visible. Our team had done a good job of work. The navigator then shot the exact angle and the parachutist dropped straight down into the circle a weighted letter in which I told Brézillon the parachuting operations would begin at seven o'clock the next morning.

A few minutes later we made a perfect landing at Djanet airstrip where I met the officers of the post as well as Lesage.

The next day was devoted to the preparation of the containers. Vasseur, a specialist in such matters, looked after this; he separated

the supplies into lots and put one of each into a basketwork re-
ceptacle which he strapped up and then carefully fastened to
a parachute. All that is not as easy as it sounds and, in fact, requires
a great deal of experience if it is to be well done. Then, suddenly
Vasseur stopped dead: there were only eight parachutes—and
there were no less than fourteen packages. So it was decided
that six packages should just be dropped, therefore poor Vasseur
had to undo all his work so as to take out the foodstuffs which
would be the less likely to be damaged in a free drop. Flour,
noodles, dried vegetables, salt and soap were sorted out and then
stuffed into big sacks well lined with straw.

On the appointed day at seven o'clock we flew over Sefar and
saw, on the dropping area, our companions who had come to
light the smoke-fuses under the eyes of the puzzled Tuareg. I sent
down a weighted message to say that six packages, contrary to
programme, would be dropped without parachutes and that
therefore the terrain must be evacuated during the operation.

We took a broad swoop over Sefar and reached the dropping
area. The door of the plane had been taken off and everyone on
board was at his post. The packages to be dropped were attached
by snap-hooks to a central cable that ran the whole length of the
fuselage; all that had to be done was to push them one after another
out into the air. Mothe, the co-pilot, at the rear, in touch by
telephone with the controls where Captain Flachard and I were
sitting, supervised the operation and reported to us what was
happening.

Then, at the very moment when the first package dropped, we
noticed that the members of our expedition were still on the
terrain, so the captain, very prudently, gave orders to hold things
up; then we executed another manœuvre. We flew at 300 feet,
the altitude for dropping operations. These sweeps over the sun-

L

scorched rocks of Sefar were exciting enough, but the spectacle must be absolutely entrancing farther up, where the huge forest of rock seesaws over the whole horizon.

We flew back over the terrain and were relieved to see that our people were just getting away from the marked area. After he had calculated his angle of release and had given the usual warnings, the captain pressed with one hand on the catch that worked the siren. That was the signal. The plane dipped a wing and the package, pushed by Vasseur, dropped off into space. The displacement of air raised a cloud of dust and our parachutist would certainly have been sucked out if he had not been wearing a belt fastened to the central cable.

The package bumped to the ground on the eastern edge of the terrain while we saw an immense cloud arise and our terrified lads making off as fast as their legs would carry them.

Mothe shouted to us by micro:

'That was flour and the sack's burst.'

'Damn,' answered Flachard. 'The cords must have been too tight. I'll drop down a bit.'

Under us a long white track ripped through the ground which, if it had not been well enough marked out before, certainly was now. But how was it that Brézillon and his companions had not cleared off the area as they had been told? I hoped that this time they would understand.

Five times the manœuvre was repeated and the droppers, for Guichard and Lesage were helping Vasseur, were kept very busy. Hardly had one load gone overboard than the plane circled round over the terrain once more and the siren began to shriek in the fuselage. All the packages fell, without mishap, well within the dropping area.

The captain said that as the dropping operation was finished he was going up to 600 feet for the parachuting. However, for a little time we hovered at about 450 feet so as to let drop a third weighted message announcing the parachuting of the eight remaining loads.

'Look out! Ready?'

The siren screamed once again and the plane dipped one wing a little. A very slight shock and then a magnificent red corolla burst into blossom in the air and floated gracefully down to the ground. The parachute was carried away a little to one side by the wind that was rather strong, as the smoke-fuses showed. Obviously this time Brézillon had got my message all right. However, the parachute took some time to land and the men seemed to have some trouble in getting it to the ground.

We sent down a second and a third container. This time the parachutes were white. Then we heard a noise in the rear, the lieutenant had just reported:

'Parachute suspending-ropes snapped during drop; container crashed on ground.'

'Well,' said Flachard, 'you can be sure that from this height everything has been smashed to smithereens.'

I cast my eye over the manifest and saw that container No. 5 held sugar, flour, salt and noodles. Then I looked downwards; a huge star-shaped splotch showed how violent had been the impact—and also how great the damage.

The three following containers got down safely, then the last parachute, green in colour, spread open and the operation was over. I must say that the whole thing had been conducted in masterly fashion, and even if two loads had crashed the rude, rough carcass of the Tassili was largely to blame. Moreover, such incidents are inevitable in operations of this kind.

As it was, the result was most gratifying to us of the expedition, since we now had two and a half months' supplies and for the first time enjoyed a really plentiful stock of potatoes, oranges, onions, bacon, salt cod and so forth, not to mention ready-for-use desserts, jams and cakes which served to enliven meals that had become really too monotonous and insipid to be bearable.

A last glance at the plateau slipping away from underneath us as the captain opened out the throttle. After having described a magnificent sweep over the stony forests, he zoomed up. As we were carrying practically no weight the occupants of the fuselage who had not been warned—and who had not seen the grin on the captain's face now that he could at last let himself go—found themselves all huddled together in a struggling mass at the bottom of the cockpit. Guichard almost swallowed his pipe and Lesage found a bump rising on his forehead. I do not know which one of them it was who, at this moment, hit on the idea of utilizing a little funnel that hung within reach on the side of the plane. Whoever it was he seemed to have thought that the thing was a speaking-tube, but it was not, and luckily before he had opened his mouth to talk, he suddenly realized that the instrument was designed to relieve the needs of nature felt by the crew. Well, in Army planes everything has to be arranged so as to economize space.

Now we were quietly munching on some sandwiches and chatting away while our droppers, who had got over their rough-and-tumble surprise, were beaming with delight at the thought of their adventure.

As we went we made out the route we were to fly over the next day in order to take the air photographs. I indicated the way first over the magnificent Tamrit canyon, then over the *akba* of Aroum. We made a reconnaissance of the Aouanrhet and Jabbaren massifs (the Tassili looks so easy from above!) and then went as far as Iherir, where we turned back and made a bee-line for Djanet.

During this time Lajoux jogged along as fast as his legs would carry him toward the Tafalelet *akba*. He was laden with his camera and rolls of film that had been exposed during the parachuting operations and must be developed as soon as possible. A meeting had been arranged for eight o'clock that evening at the foot of the *akba* where a jeep from the Annex was to wait for him and then take him to Djanet.

It was about ten o'clock when he got to the mess and began to tell us how the various phases of the parachuting appeared to him on the ground. It seemed that enthusiasm reigned in our camp. The operation had excited everyone and they could hardly contain themselves at the thought of the sensational meals we should be able to prepare. The Tuaregs, so he said, had been absolutely stupefied at watching the parachutes drift down from the sky . . . an event that would long be talked about in the Tassili.

By seven o'clock the next morning we were off by plane once more. Lajoux had his cameras strapped about him. The day before we had tried to take vertical views, that is to say, ones straight down as seen from the trapdoor that opened in the floor of the plane. Scherlé, the photographer, had to lie at full length on his belly and put his head outside while Guichard and Lesage grabbed on to his feet so that he should not slip or be sucked out by the terrific pull of the air current. The poor fellow's position was dreadfully uncomfortable while the heavy camera he had slung round his neck was difficult to handle. It was obvious that he would never be able to get really good pictures if he had to maintain such a disagreeable position, that is to say, one with, practically speaking, a third of his body hanging out into the void. The danger, indeed, appeared so great that I called the thing off.

We had to be satisfied with slanting views taken from the unscrewed window of the door. Lajoux filmed all the massifs with paintings, but he had to break off his work several times since the dipping of the wings and the dancing of the plane in air-pockets made him feel sick. All the same, we got more than two hundred views of different parts of the Tassili and they form quite a good collection which complements the pictures we took on the ground.

We flew as far as Iherir to photograph a little agricultural area that contains a number of small lakes; some of them are as much as 1000 yards long and they are the largest in all the Sahara. Captain Rossi had told me about a huge pre-Islamic monument between Iherir and Aharar. We had no difficulty in spotting it. It stands on the slope of a peak and impressed us by its unusual size for it appeared to be more than a hundred yards in diameter. In form it is a great oval and we noticed inside it rows of stones arranged in what, to us, looked like the outline of a keyhole. According to the Tuareg this structure is the tomb of an ancient queen of their country. We managed to get some pictures of the 'mausoleum'. We were able to note the presence round about of many other similar tombs (if that is what they are) but of smaller dimensions; these monuments always face the east and occur in quite arid areas while we came across none near the paintings. It is possible that the 'tombs' have no connection at all with the prehistoric pictures.

This air reconnaissance also enabled me to understand in a few minutes what I had been unable to make out (because of the lack of any general view of the country) from the ground, that is to say, the structure of the Tassili. I had always wondered why it was possible to find on the plateau—which, after all, is of one geological formation—some areas that are flat, others that are massifs eroded into dome-like shapes and still others which are cut up into colonnades of sandstone—and so forth. The fact is that all the Tassili sandstones presented, originally, the same chequer structure which, according to some geologists, is due to lateral compression. This chequer structure is still visible in its primitive form in several places, and it is very easily recognizable from the air though hardly perceptible when one is on the ground. Erosion has, for the most part, been most marked on the main lines of the Tassili chequer-board for these must have presented areas of least resistance. With the passage of time these lines became eroded and scooped out down to various depths so there was produced a quadrangular sort of fretwork reminding one rather of a rice cake which has been cut up into regular-shaped pieces. According as the erosion has been more or less intense, the sandstone has assumed, superficially, different forms which vary from the chequer-board plateau, through masses with very rounded summits and then through very thick-set and jagged forests of rocks to needles farther apart from one another. These last constitute the product of erosion's penultimate phase, the last of which is evidenced in the destruction of the needles and their wearing down to mere stumps. As all these different types of rock-formation exist side by side the Tassili presents a most varied character, for we never came across two massifs which were alike. The chequer-board construction also explains why we always had the impression of being in ruined cities with squares, main highways and secondary streets. The structure also allows us to understand why the Tassili was always, in ancient times, so suitable for human settlement—and why as a consequence of such settlement we found there so many rock-paintings.

It is a pleasingly paradoxical thought that it is aeroplanes, the most modern of inventions, which allow us to illuminate the problems of the past.

16

Mission Accomplished

Now that Lesage had joined us and Guichard had come back we were able to carry out our whole programme of work at Sefar. All the area was divided up, each one took up his appointed task and we all painted away at our copies. It seemed at times a thankless task, and it was always a harassing one, often hampered, for several days on end, by the sand winds that prevented us from making tracings and forced us to lay down our paint-brushes. The onset of the great heat is generally accompanied in the Tassili by very high winds. Two storms descended upon us and transformed the *wadi* into a roaring torrent—and also filled up our pools, whose level had sunk perilously low.

Lajoux took advantage of the calmer weather to photograph and film the most picturesque nooks and recesses of the Sefar area. One day he wandered off our usual tracks and walked towards a group of rocks where, up to then, we had been able to make out nothing at all. His attention was attracted by a huge spread of brownish colour, but its shape gave no indication of what it might once have been intended to represent. Still, the thing aroused his curiosity, so when he got back to camp he recruited three others of the team and the four of them went off to wash this particular rock-wall. Once again swabbing did the trick, and soon the four young fellows were gazing open-mouthed at an image taking shape before their eyes. Quite by chance they had discovered a

61 and 62. *Tin-Abou Teka: War Chariot: Period of the 'Flying Gallop' Chariots*

63. *Ala-n-Edoument: War Chariot: Period of the 'Flying Gallop' Chariots* ▶

64. *Adjefou: 'Bi-triangular' Men: Period of the 'Flying Gallop' Chariots and of Mounted Horses*   Preceding double-page spread

65. *Adjefou: The Large Giraffe: Various Periods*

66. *Adjefou: Giraffe Hunt: Period of Mounted Horses*

67. *Adjefou: Ostriches and Antelopes: 'Round Heads' Period*

68. *Adjefou: Animal-headed Hunters: Bovidian Period*

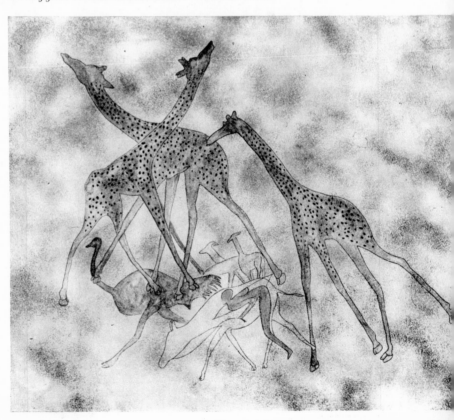

69. *Ouan Abou: Giraffes Fighting: Bovidian Period*

masterpiece which will take its place among the most beautiful paintings of all time.

The subject? A man and a woman, nothing more.

But a most remarkable man and an even more remarkable woman. She is depicted life-size, in red ochre, and she is sitting facing her companion. Her body, held proudly erect, has a bended head. The bust is of magnificent proportions and the figure is well defined. The whole admirably balanced. The breasts somewhat heavy and rounded are those of a woman who has already suckled a child. One of the legs is stretched out, the other is bent backwards so that the harmonious curves of the knees and the delicately formed ankles are well displayed.

It is, indeed, a painting of rare perfection and one that by its superb rendering of the human form is worthy to be compared with the sculpture of ancient Greece or with the works of the Renaissance artists.

By their size these two figures are imposing. We were filled with astonishment and admiration that such a masterpiece should have been painted by Stone Age men. And what Stone Age men were the creators of this magnificent picture?

The 'Bovidians'. . . . When, later on, all our copies are arranged together and when art critics and specialists have had time to examine them at their leisure, I am certain they will admit that our 'Bovidian' artists were undisputed masters of a naturalistic art. Here we have not just reproductions of animals, the 'Bovidian' painters also took as models human figures and no one before them had done this on the same scale. That is to say, our Tassili prehistoric artists made a new contribution to the whole history of art and they will henceforth take a high place among the great precursors.

A few more weeks of work and then we should be able, with a light heart, to leave the marvellous rocks of Sefar's impressive prehistoric settlement, because we could be sure that we had left nothing undiscovered behind us; nothing uncopied either, for we had reproduced all the paintings in the Tassili except for one 'Abominable Sand Man' who was so large that an attempt to copy him was prevented by insoluble technical problems.

During the last few days of our stay I sent Guichard and Lajoux to Tahilali, there to copy the paintings in a grotto discovered in 1950. At the same time they were to visit the nearby agricultural area of Iherir with its many pools of water. One had to allow for ten days' march over a rather dreary plateau. Jebrin was the guide, and the little caravan, with a month's foodstuffs, made its way by Ti-n-Bedjedj and the Oued Iddo. However, a stupid and ridiculous incident soon held up our travellers. One fine morning, indeed, a badly broken-in camel threw the convoy into confusion and so startled all the other animals that they chucked off their loads with great violence on to the ground. The drawing-table, the cameras, a radio-set that Guichard had brought from Algiers, sacks of food, water-skins, everything was scattered about in disorder over a hundred square yards. The place looked like a battlefield. To make matters worse, the guilty beast had made off and Jebrin swore he could not catch it again. But, it so happened, quite by chance of course, that some Tuareg encampments were not far away. Moreover, in three days' time there was to be a marriage which was to be attended by all the Kel Medak for miles around, about a hundred people in all. Jebrin maintained that it was quite impossible to find another camel to take the place of the deserter. . . . Obviously the whole business was a put-up affair and our guide had the firm intention of spending the following few days feasting with the people of the country. Guichard and Lajoux, however, were completely taken in by the excellent stage-management.

So our two young men hurried on to the feast, where for days and nights they gorged themselves with boiled goats' meat and wheaten cakes to the intoxicating rhythm of the tomtoms. Result: the little party got to Iherir a week late.

Iherir is a singular little oasis for the Tassili and it is inhabited by a few dozen families of mixed Negro and Tuareg stock, each one of which cultivates its own plot of ground. There are palms, many fig-trees and even some vines. This isolated agricultural community is, indeed, the best supplied with water of any in central Sahara. Moreover, what would be unthinkable elsewhere, pools follow on one after another in the bed of the *wadi*, some of them a thousand yards long and thirty or forty feet deep.

The little lakes are full of fish and, in former days, I made there some astonishingly copious catches which provided me with an excellent fry. But it was not the fish which, this time, attracted my companions to the shores of the pools. While the natives stood about perplexed and wondering what the white men would do next, Guichard, Lajoux and Jebrin busied themselves with a mysterious bundle of sticks they had taken off a camel's back. The sticks were fitted together and before long were transformed into a kind of framework with pointed ends and on to which a covering of cloth and rubber was slipped. Jebrin was exceptionally cheerful, even for him, especially when the Tuareg around him suddenly saw floating in the water a strange, fragile-looking craft which, adroitly handled by Guichard, shot gaily across the surface of the water and skimmed across the lake like an arrow.

At once the whole village collected and cried aloud in enthusiasm. Surely the French must have signed a pact with the devil, else how could they be so clever? Not only had they brought down tons of supplies from the air (for the news of our parachute operation had travelled fast), but now they were paddling about on the water like ducks—for these birds, during their migrations, sometimes alight at Iherir. The excitement of the people reached its climax when the two *rumis* made a dive and frisked about in the water they had longed for during weeks and months. To the Tuareg—who do not know how to swim—the spectacle was a rare one indeed, and Jebrin roared with laughter and shouted '*Agaru, agaru kufar*', that is, 'Frog, Christian frog'.

But Guichard and Lajoux did not stop at this exhibition of their skill as oarsmen and swimmers. I had asked them to find out if there were still any crocodiles at Iherir. The object of the little observation *kayak* which I had used on the Niger and on some of the small bodies of water in the Hoggar, was to enable my companions to inspect all the creeks and rock-pools in Iherir which cannot be reached on foot. Iherir is, indeed, the last place in which crocodiles are reported to have lingered. During the first French explorations of the Tassili, Captain Touchard had noted at Iherir plenty of traces of these reptiles, while, when two years later, Captain Niéger visited the region one of his N.C.O.s actually killed a crocodile whose remains may be seen to this day in the zoological laboratory of Algiers University. The creature was hardly more than six feet long. Another specimen shot by Lieutenant Beauval, in 1924, was about the same length. Obviously these beasts did not eat hearty meals every day—hence their small size. But the astonishing thing is that they managed to have survived at all in these lakes and until quite recent times. It is, in fact, a most extraordinary thing that crocodiles, whose fondness for red meat is well known, should have lived on for centuries despite what must have been undernourishment, but that these reptiles did survive is conclusive evidence of the Sahara's damp past and of times when a vast system of rivers cut through the country from north to south and linked the fauna of the Tunisian *chotts* (*see* p. 18) with that of the Niger and Lake Chad.

Today in the lonely lakes of Iherir the only food a crocodile can find is fish eked out, from time to time, with a goat or a dog that may venture too near when it comes to drink . . . but the Tuareg are ever on the alert and do not let their animals wander about alone.

In 1934 and 1935 I visited the different pools but I did not catch sight of even the tip of a crocodile's nose, and it was in vain that I searched for tracks or droppings. The local inhabitants assured me that there were no more crocodiles at all in their lakes, and that the last of these reptiles was the one shot by Beauval in 1924. I thought, however, that, since crocodiles grow very slowly, some little ones might easily have escaped the natives' notice and therefore a new prospection of the area was desirable. But neither Guichard nor Lajoux could get any satisfactory information, so the outing was for them just a pleasant experience on and in the water—and not everyone can say that he has rowed a boat on and swum about in a Saharan lake.

Now we had come to the end of our adventure and we all gathered together at Sefar. Michel Brézillon and Vila—whom I had sent off to Ala-n-Edoument, had got back and we set to work to make lists of the copies executed and to put the finishing touches to our reports. Tables and ladders were dismounted and packed away in their cases, all the supplies were put into boxes and each one of us prepared his own luggage. Oh, I hasten to say that these bags of ours were not heavy or cumbersome; no, what was tricky to deal with were the stone artefacts, the pottery fragments, the botanical specimens and so forth which we had accumulated over a term of months. We threw away what seemed of no use, we classified, we arranged, and we abandoned, not without regret, such things as a worn-out pair of sandals, a tattered shirt, an old can-opener, a bit of broken looking-glass or an improvised pipe-cleaner made out of a piece of wire; poor things no longer of any value or use, but all the same things which, during our sojourn in a deserted land, had often proved serviceable.

We walked about; we looked to see if we had forgotten anything; we went off and sat near the shelters, there to gaze for the last time on the frescoes, to feel the warm air in sand-choked corridors where so very often we had stumbled along with a table on our backs; we went to say good-bye to the wild olive by the *wadi*, the tree whose blossoming we had awaited so jealously for months; we did not forget to cast a tender glance at the little flower blooming among the rocks. We all wanted to survey our domain. With an eagerness that may easily be understood we had looked forward to the day when we should leave the haunts of prehistoric man and return once more to civilized life. . . . Now that this day was at hand our hearts were heavy.

Our donkeys were there, the Tuareg also; they had assembled for a last journey. We looked at them in a strange way. Something about them seemed to be changed. We realized that a fraternal bond had been forged, a bond that had united us for long months. Poor donkeys, so often beaten because they did not move along fast enough, all at once we liked to look at their long, mobile ears, their furtively intelligent eyes. We found our asses attractive; indeed, we were surprised to feel that we almost loved them. Jebrin, Agaoued and Rissa held themselves more gravely than usual—they knew that this was the end of a great adventure.

Round the camp-fire that night, if conversation turned on preparations for departure, thoughts were elsewhere. We did not talk about what most filled our minds, but each one of us feasted his eyes for the last time on a vision of great rocks which, under the moonlight, stood out on the horizon and reached up like black lace into the July night towards the thousand shooting stars that ripped across the firmament.

It is time to leave. Rissa has collected his grimy pots and pans.

Jebrin and Agaoued had finished loading the twelve donkeys. The little hooves hammered on the sandstone blocks of the *wadi*'s right bank. Guichard, puffing on his pipe as usual, went ahead with Jebrin. Vila, his cameras still slung about him, followed with a stick in his hand. He looked a good deal more alert than when he had arrived. His belly had disappeared. Michel, who walked beside him, also sported a cudgel and advanced with his head bent down watching the stones, while Lajoux rushed about backwards and forwards photographing all the time as though he meant to record for posterity every detail of the scene. None of us spoke a word, though from time to time we would cast longing looks towards the stony horizon hiding the stage on which we had played our parts in a singular experience. Each man was wondering whether he would ever see such things again or whether fate would make him a minor civil servant and a respectable father of a family who would sit, in the evening, with slippered feet by the fireside.

The descent of the Tafalelet *akba* jerked us back to the present. The donkeys' loads slipped and we had to help the animals along. No more time for melancholy. Once more the gorges filled with the echoes of a thousand noises . . . Jebrin, or Rissa or Guichard calling for help and the rumble of stony cascades tumbling down from beneath the little asses' hooves.

Then came the Taramit, the doleful *reg* and the granite rocks which that day gave off terrific heat so that this part of our journey left us one of the most disagreeable memories of all our expedition. Djanet at last, and the Dar Diaf, close to which the caravan stopped for good. Once they are freed from their burdens the donkeys are quite frisky. One by one, led by Agaoued shouting and yelling at the more wayward animals, they go down the slope of the *bordj*.

It was on this last scene that fell the curtain of our sixteen months' drama.

So, what I had glimpsed during my early weeks of prospection in the Tassili had been fully verified. The region is, indeed, as far as we know today, the richest centre of prehistoric art in the whole world. Our balance-sheet is, in this connection, convincing: 800 rock-paintings were copied, and these, if joined up, would cover a surface of over one thousand five hundred square yards. These are the bare figures, but they do not convey the contribution that the Tassili frescoes make to the history of art and to our knowledge of ancient African cultures. Furthermore, what the figures do not indicate is the price paid for these prizes. The achievement of the members of the expedition is all the more remarkable in that none of them had had any previous training in Saharan life. Moreover, they performed cheerfully the humblest tasks, they put up with physical conditions which were very trying, they worked without respite, day after day, in a fierce climate, in a region entirely isolated and deprived of all resources.

Of course, I would not pretend that what my companions did can be compared with very perilous mountaineering or with some subterranean explorations—these are more spectacular, more in the nature of sporting feats. Our adventure had nothing theatrical about it, it was even, one may say, disappointing in its monotony. But it may not be easy to imagine just what efforts were demanded of our team. Well, one may say, a daily transport of drawing-tables and ladders, an intensive labour in the depths of grottoes, and every day the same eternal dish of noodles . . . What of it? But I will ask you to think of such a life lasting, without respite, for sixteen months during which we were, to all intents and purposes, cut off from the rest of the world.

There is a word that comes to my mind, one which I might well use to characterize the spirit in which our team performed their tasks, but I would rather leave it to others to say. There are apparently little efforts which, repeated every day, demand from a man more resistance, more moral courage, more physical strength than some of the most spectacular sporting achievements. Our reward—and for me, at least, it is the most satisfying of any my Saharan life has won me—is that of having contributed to the annals of mankind a mass of documentation which is, of its sort, unique, for it relates to the message, thousands of years old, left by peoples unknown up to now. It is a message of life, of art and of Man's universal character. A message, it seems to me, that cannot fail to move us deeply.

M

17

Did We Discover Atlantis?

A s soon as our discoveries were made known, they caused a great sensation in many different spheres. The revelation that the Sahara hid evidence of cultures long since disappeared came at about the same time that the desert was much in the news because of the oil and other mineral wealth to be found there.

It seemed to many rather a curious coincidence that evidence concerning the Sahara's past should have been found simultaneously with proof of what its future may be. So, in the space of a few weeks, the desert, considered to be one of the most arid and forlorn of all the world's regions, and as one which might interest a few half-crazy scientists or a handful of millionaire tourists looking for an exciting experience, this Sahara stood revealed as an area of topical interest.

Our discoveries did not fail to surprise many people. A discovery of prehistoric man's traces was one thing, but it was altogether unprecedented that there should be found a great number of frescoes presenting such varied and novel subjects. Nothing more, indeed, was needed to excite rumours of forgery, very discreet rumours, of course—just whispered. Still, these allegations were so much waste of breath for no one cared to follow them up. What a fine thing it would have been for us to have had our Rouffignac in the Tassili.

On the other hand, several people who saw our copies made reserves about some of the figures whose style seemed so modern that the authenticity of the copies aroused doubts. Such doubts, I hasten to add, were not made in any malicious spirit but in a laudable attempt at constructive criticism.

But, alas for these over-zealous critics, we shall not have our Rouffignac, or our Glozel, or our Piltdown or our Moulin-Quignon,[1] all names celebrated in the stormy annals of prehistory. And the reason is that there is not a single forgery—intentional or unintentional—in the paintings and copies we brought back from the Tassili.

Still, I must confess that we did do a little forgery, for we painted in red ochre on sandstone slabs a number of little human figures treated in the 'Bovidian' manner. These slivers when they were moved from Djanet to Paris completely puzzled and hoaxed most of the specialists who saw them. We had, indeed, made these paintings without any ulterior motive and with no thought of deceiving anyone. We just wanted to find out how pigment held on and was applied to a sandstone surface.

It all began with our running out of *gouache* pigment and our being forced to utilize the local ochres, that is to say ochreous schists found on the spot and identical with those employed by the prehistoric Tassili artists. From our experiments we learned two things: first of all, that these schists did yield the same colours and produce the same substances as those of the rupestral pictures, and, secondly, we discovered that there was no difficulty in painting on sandstone, rather the sandstones absorb colour better than drawing-paper and to such an extent that the brush leaves no

[1] Rouffignac is a painted cavern in the south-west of France, the authenticity of whose 'prehistoric' paintings has been much called in question. Glozel was the site of a particularly impudent and clumsy mass of forged pottery and other 'prehistoric' remains. The Moulin-Quignon jaw is that of a modern *Homo sapiens*, but which for long was held by some to be of remote antiquity.

smudges on the stone. Here, then, was the explanation of the
surprisingly delicate lines, those downstrokes and thin strokes
which had filled us with admiration for the prehistoric artists. So
there was no more mystery about the technique of the Tassili
painters, and this Guichard had demonstrated by amusing himself
and by making the very fine-looking 'prehistoric paintings' on
pieces of sandstone.

So, that is our confession, that is how we became forgers. If
some time in the future, by some odd chance, in the sales-rooms or
in a dealer's shop, a museum or an art-collector is offered for a
few million francs a Tassili prehistoric sandstone slab, let the
buyer beware and before he pays let him put the thing under the
water-tap. If the paint is fast then he can pay without hesitation
(though maybe he should first look under the microscope at the
surface of the stone so as to see whether or not it is covered by a
layer of transparent lacquer put on by some cunning Chinese
artificer), but if the paint washes off in the water, the prospective
purchaser should show the vendor to the door. The thing will
be a forgery, or rather a pseudo-forgery, for there are real forgeries
and false forgeries—the terminology varies according to the
intention of the forger!

Here, however, is the essence of what I want to say. It will
always be easy enough to determine whether a Tassili fresco is
authentic or false. All you have to do is to swab down the rock-
face. All prehistoric paintings with a red-ochre base have so deeply
penetrated into the substance of the stone that they are now
indelible. The yellow ochres on the other hand (often applied,
especially in some figures of the 'Martian' type, in thick coats) are
not so stable, although they do resist water quite well. The whites,
however, are much more delicate and must be treated with care.
Since it is not often that yellow ochre or whites are used alone in
the Tassili pictures, it is, practically speaking, always possible to

find out whether a painting is ancient or not. In any case, a small portion of the surface if removed and placed under a microscope will reveal oxidization in depth. The Tassili pictures can never give rise to the epic combats which aroused so much excitement concerning the Rouffignac discoveries.

The reactions I have just mentioned were not, of course, the only ones aroused by our pictures. Indeed, during our stay in the Tassili we had a great many letters which were one of our main sources of amusement when we were not working. We got, indeed, letters bearing stamps of all colours and postmarks of every imaginable country. Some of these communications were perfectly serious and came from scientific institutions or from foreign scientists. Other missives, however, were much more fanciful. Several of our correspondents would have that our 'Martians' were really 'Jupi-terrestrials' [*sic*], and that our boasted 'revelations' were nothing but mere confirmations of knowledge long since acquired by the 'initiates' of some theosophical sect or other, 'knowledge' which 'official' scientists (in which class I was honoured with a place) had as yet not understood, nor ever would understand.

Again, some writers—and these were the most enthusiastic —did not hesitate to state that we had resuscitated Atlantis and thus had settled all the controversies which have caused so much ink to be spilt ever since Plato himself had recounted the story of Atlantis in his celebrated Dialogues, the *Critias* and the *Timaeus*.

'Atlantis, that's it—it's the works of the Atlantes you've just discovered. The remains are those of the famed submerged island destroyed by the ire of the gods and you've set foot there without knowing it. You have revealed that Plato's story was not just a fable.'

Some of the correspondents were kind enough to credit me

with the gift of prophecy. When I went to the Tassili, I knew, of course, quite well where I was going. I had had the right idea and therefore I had found what I sought.

It is hardly necessary for me to state that I never said or wrote anything of the kind either before, during or after our discovery of the Tassili rock-paintings. If I gave the name of 'Antinea' to the charming female figure painted on a Jabbaren rock-wall, well, that was just because I yielded to a romantic whim caused no doubt by memories of the celebrated heroine in Pierre Benoit's novel; her name is, in the minds of generations of men, associated with Atlantis and the Hoggar, of which latter mountain mass the Tassili is, after all, only a prolongation.

I would add that in his book Benoit's role as a magician is a double one. True, Atlantis had been much discussed before 'Antinea' was written, but by taking the ancient fable as part of the groundwork of his book, Benoit gave wide publicity to the Atlantis story, though it may well be doubted if he ever thought he would excite, in France and in other countries, both a spate of Atlantis literature and also new researches into the old legend.

All the same, if, during the past thirty years, Atlantis literature has much increased, still, what we may call 'Atlantomania' is no new thing. Ever since Plato's time, the exuberant imagination of all sorts of visionaries has been at work endeavouring to resuscitate the Atlantis myth. And imagination has been matched by unlimited ingenuousness wedded to crass ignorance. Indeed, a nineteenth-century scientist, Susemehl, was moved to write that 'a list of the opinions ventilated about Atlantis would make an excellent contribution to the history of human folly'.

However, if we exclude a few theories which were not always by any means ingenuous and which in fact came perilously near to imposture, it is certain that Plato's statements have had the positive

effect of stimulating research on the part of reputable scientists
who have made use, successively, of oceanography, geology,
anthropology and ethnology in their enquiries. We may say, then,
that the subject is a formidable one and should engage all our
ardent 'Atlantophiles' in the paths of prudence.

However, it is not surprising that the most ardent of such
enthusiasts do not know—or, anyway, do not understand—the
reliable work done in this field by men of science. Naturally enough,
it is always more amusing to move about in an atmosphere of fable
than to tire one's eyes puzzling over texts that are often for-
bidding enough.

As Imbelloni has written, 'both philosophers and philanthropists
have found in Atlantis climate and surroundings most suited for
the children of their fancies, a Utopia all the more attractive since
it has never had any existence'.

A place that is nowhere and everywhere. If we follow, indeed,
the lead of the many authors who have dealt with the question—
their names would be wearisome to quote—we must note with
alarm that Atlantis has been located in the Sea of Azov, in Lake
Tritonis, in the two Gulfs of Syrtis, in the island of Djerba, the
Canaries, Andalusia, Greenland, the environs of Cadiz, Morocco,
the Baetic peninsula, the former Iceland-Armorican continent,
Spitzbergen, Newfoundland, Nigeria—and that does not exhaust
the list for the New World as well as the Old has its partisans.

It was, during the last century, Professor Berlioux of Lyons
University who was the first to mention the Sahara in connection
with 'Atlantis'. It is he, moreover, disguised as 'Professor Le Mège'
who served as Benoit's model for the old bookworm who discovered the lost passages of the *Critias* in Antinea's library. Benoit's
novel aroused the imagination of a German geologist, one
Borchardt, who situated Atlantis in the region of the Tunisian

chotts and in the Hoggar. Borchardt's theories gave rise to the following nightmarish adventure. In 1925, when the Abalessa fort was being excavated,[1] there was exhumed the skeleton of a woman, identified as a Berber 'queen' by the name of Ti-Hinan, whom the Tuareg look upon as their ancestress. An American millionaire, who took part in the dig, did not hesitate to broadcast to the world that the skeleton was that of Antinea—not in flesh but in bone—the last queen of the people of Atlantis. Now, the tomb in question dates back only to the fourth century A.D., so Ti-Hinan must have been pretty long-lived and have possessed an exception-ally robust constitution if she survived during the 700 years from the time of Plato (who died in 347 B.C.) to the fourth century of our era. But even so, the count is not right, for we have to fit in the 900 years which had elapsed before Plato wrote of the Atlantis drama. Maybe the American was not very convinced about his own discovery, since a news item that appeared three or four years ago in the world's Press announced that, with the aid of asdic, he was going to look for traces of Atlantis near the Azores. Apparently the search has not, up to now, been very suc-cessful, for nothing further about his activities seems to have been reported.

The fact is that there is no possibility whatsoever of the Sahara having been the site of Plato's mysterious island. The text clearly attributes the destruction of Atlantis to phenomena of tectonic and not of diluvial origin. There was an earthquake that rent the island asunder before it sank beneath the waves. If that was what happened then we should be able to find traces of such a sub-sidence, but what we know of the geology of the Sahara is quite enough to show that there has not been there any subsidence or invasion of the sea; on the contrary, there has been uplift. One

[1] I mention Abalessa on p. 130 when dealing with the question of the Romans in the central Sahara. (Author's note.)

70. The Tassili Barrier in the Region of Tafalelet
71. The Stone 'Forest' in the Region of Tamrit, Ti-n-Bedjadj

might add, however, that this uplift occurred long before Man made his appearance on this globe of ours.

During the last few years prehistorical research has made much progress and this confirms, furthermore, that the Atlantic and Moroccan coasts of Africa have been stable since at least the beginning of the Quaternary Period. Not only have traces of human life been found on the shores (and relating to populations living on the produce of the soil), but, in addition, there have been discovered round the Canaries cordons of shells identical with those on the Moroccan coasts—a proof that the general shape of those islands and of the continent's shores has not changed for tens of thousands of years. Again, the ancient life of the African continent, and especially of the Sahara, is illustrated in prehistoric sites. There are to be found everywhere ancient industries— Chelleo-Acheulian, Levalloisian, Mousterian, and although Upper Palaeolithic seems to be wanting, neolithic artefacts are so abundant that they seem to indicate that few regions of the earth could have been more thickly populated than the Sahara in neolithic times.

All these deposits are in their right places, that is to say, where the ancient populations left them both on the coasts and in the interior.

This state of things indicates that the Saharan platform has remained stable ever since the appearance of their earliest hominids[1] and that the whole area has suffered neither uplift nor subsidence for many hundreds of thousands of years. These are facts which the 'Saharan' Atlantophiles should take into account, since this evidence reduces to nonsense the pleasing hypothesis about the famous 'Red Men' in whom some have seen the Atlantes

[1] I translate *hommes* here by 'hominid' rather than by 'men', since, although the makers of e.g. Chellean and Acheulian artefacts were undoubtedly 'men' they were 'men' of a sort unlike ourselves and the word 'men' for most non-specialist readers probably suggests *Homo sapiens*.

72. The Needles to the North of Sefar

considered as the originators both of the Mexican high cultures and of the Nile Valley civilization!

As a matter of fact there are two problems, first that of the men of Atlantis and then that of Atlantis itself, for the starting-point of the whole legend consists of two texts, the first, and more ancient, of which is that of Herodotus, while the second, and more recent, is that of Plato.

In a chapter about the peoples of Libya, Herodotus mentions the Atlantes among the populations inhabiting, first, the regions to the west of the Nile (in the immediate vicinity of the coasts and going from east to west) and, second, the regions lying to the south of the first area and therefore situated in the interior of the country. Thus it is that he put the Garamantes in the heart of the Fezzan where was their capital Garama (that has been identified with the present-day town of Jerma). Then, according to Herodotus, came, ten days' march off, the Atarantes, and, again another ten days' march away, the Atlantes who lived on the Atlas Mountains.

This text of Herodotus has given rise to many interpretations, but now that the geography of the Sahara is quite well known, the identification of sites does not present insoluble problems, especially as the Greek historian took the trouble to provide relatively precise descriptions of the regions he mentioned. He speaks, in particular, of salt domes and of houses built of blocks of salt, and he adds the remark that the Libyans should count themselves lucky that they have no rain, since if a shower fell then their houses would melt away.

Now it is a well-established fact that the low-lying regions of the Sahara are saturated with salt and that the houses built near such Fezzan oases as In-Salah, and so forth, would, at the slightest fall of rain, fade away like snow under the sun's rays. Such an observation as that about the salt proves that Herodotus had at his disposal very accurate information. It is, indeed, remarkable that he mentions, in connection with the Lands of the South, salt domes, a geological formation very characteristic of the desert. From where did he get such reliable intelligence? Very probably from the caravan men who visited the Fezzan oases and who, like their descendants today, were accustomed to describe the situation of any given place by stating the number of days' march necessary from one point to another.

Ten days' march, then, from the Garamantes were the Atarantes—who, therefore, must have lived in the Tassili. Ten days farther on were the Atlas Mountains with their inhabitants the Atlantes. If we take a day's march to be twenty-five miles, then the Atlantes would have inhabited the Hoggar. But who were these Atlantes?

Herodotus writes thus about them:

'They inhabit a mountain called Atlas and it is to this mountain which they owe their name.'

That is all he tells us about their origin. It will be noted that nowhere does Herodotus speak of Atlantis, which name appears for the first time in Plato's writings, that is to say, fifty years, at least, after Herodotus.

We know that the name 'Atlas' was applied (with reference to the giant Atlas of mythology) by the Greeks to various mountains in the Peloponnese, in Sicily, in the Troad, in Ethiopia and so forth. Indeed, 'Atlas' was a fanciful, if practical, term used to designate a number of peaks, either long known or recently dis-covered. In fact, we find more and more 'Atlases' appear in one region or another as the centuries slipped by and as geographical knowledge increased. Thus, no doubt, the Hoggar received the name of Atlas which, later on, was by other authors used to desig-nate what we today call the Atlas range (in Berber *Deren*) of Morocco.

It is also evident that the word 'Atlantes' (derived from 'Atlas') was completely unknown to those peoples whom the Greeks so called.

In these circumstances it is easy to see how theories based on the words 'Atlas' and 'Atlantes' could lead to a legend of 'Atlantis'. A cardinal error was to invoke the authority of Herodotus for the situating of 'Atlantis' in Morocco, since, as we have seen, the text of the Greek historian is clear enough. He puts his 'Atlas' in the interior of Libya and not any farther to the west. Really, all he says about the regions westward from the 'Atlas' is that there could be met with still more salt domes and men as far as the Pillars of Hercules.

In comparison with this distortion of the text of Herodotus, the exaggerations of the American millionaire seem pardonable enough, for, if the Hoggar has nothing to do with Atlantis or Ti-Hinan with Antinea, all the same the Tuareg may be regarded as the descendants of those 'Atlantes' who were the contemporaries of the Father of History.

Now we come to Plato. Maybe he also was given to a little exaggeration. We know that the philosopher belonged to the Socratic School whose members professed that there were other inhabited worlds beyond the seas then known, and this belief was, it seems, not without its influence upon the Atlantis legend. Nonetheless, it was not geography that interested the Socratics but philosophical doctrines relating to the political life of men. In his works Plato endeavoured to describe what the perfect State should be. Thus it was that in the *Critias* and the *Timaeus* he gives us, as an example, the realm of the Atlantes.

Quite obviously Plato's whole account was fiction designed to strike the imagination of his listeners and readers. In order to lend more verisimilitude to his tale Plato set it in a region that was not only completely unknown but in one whose reality his audience could never either prove or disprove. Now, according to the geographical knowledge of Plato's time (that is, according to Herodotus whose works Plato must have known quite well), the Atlantes were the farthest off of any people whose name was known among those of the interior of Libya. Thus, it was simple enough to take these Atlantes as examples and to describe their social organization as though it had, in fact, reached a peak of perfection.

The disappearance of Atlantis (and the history of the island is, like all the rest of the story, purely imaginary) was willed by the gods and was a punishment inflicted upon the Atlantes for their having transgressed the rules and regulations of wise conduct.

Plato's story, furthermore, appears all the more fabulous in that he put the submergence of Atlantis at a date about a thousand years before his time, though this fact did not prevent him from describing in detail the organization of the Atlantes's army, its war-chariots, its cavalry and the rest. In this part of his tale Plato, indeed, wanders off into the frankly improbable, for we know that horses first appeared in Egypt under the Hyksōs domination (about 1800–1700 B.C.), and that they were brought from Asia, while it was not until later on that these animals made their way into Libya. The Egyptian inscriptions offer unmistakable evidence on this point. Again, as we have already noted, the Saharan rupestral engravings, in their turn, also confirm the late appearance of the horse in the Great Desert.

We may further remember that most of Plato's contemporaries disbelieved his Atlantis yarn and no other author of antiquity mentions Atlantis except in connection with Plato's account. The legend, indeed, was revived during the Middle Ages by eminent ecclesiastics who were pleased to see in the tale of the island's subsidence a phase of the biblical Flood. Later, the discovery of America gave a new lease of life to the fable, a lease that has not yet by any means run out, as is witnessed by the two thousand books and more comprising the 'Atlantis' literature.

What we were able to contribute to the problem is clear enough. To all who have asked us—sometimes with touching ingenuousness—whether we found Atlantis, I have had to say 'No'. The reason for my answer is simple. To find something, that something must exist.

18

Trial Balance

ALTHOUGH we did not find Atlantis—for obvious reasons—
we did, I think, something better. We proved that the central
Sahara was, in neolithic times, one of the most active areas
of prehistoric culture. We revealed, also, that there existed in
what is now desert, but which in far-distant times was covered with
a mantle of vegetation, many different cultures which were no
figments of the imagination at all.

Those of my readers who visited our exhibition at the Museum
of Decorative Art (the *Musée des Arts Decoratifs* in the Pavillon de
Marsan of the Louvre in Paris) must have been struck by the
splendour of the frescoes executed by the herdsmen painters of the
'Bovidian' phase. To this 'school', if I may so call it, we must give
credit for having created some of the finest specimens of what is
commonly called 'naturalistic art'. However, the most important
novelty revealed by our investigations is perhaps other.

The engravings and paintings in the Sahara seem to fall into
four main periods:

1. That of the *Bubalus*[1] hunters (early Neolithic?).
2. That of the cattle herdsmen (Neolithic).
3. That of the pastoralists with chariots and cavalry—the
so-called 'Equine Period' (Protohistoric).
4. That of the camel (dating, more or less, from the beginning
of our era).

[1] The *Bubalus* is the extinct wild buffalo of Africa (*bubalus antiquus*).

Our expedition, however, revealed that between periods 1 and 2 there comes another made up of many phases and, consequently, almost certainly, of a long duration. This discovery is a surprising, and indeed almost revolutionary, one, since, until quite recently, it was thought impossible that there could have been so many different cultures in the prehistoric Sahara.

As things appear now—for the examination of the documents has hardly begun—I calculate that we identified at least sixteen different art-phases, and at least thirty different styles—most of which antedate the 'Bovidian' period of the herdsmen. Each layer, each phase, presents, of course, its own problems. The collation and the synthesis of our documents will demand several more years' work, especially as our check-list, despite what we did on it during our sixteen months' stay, is still far from being finished. For the present we must be satisfied with a general summary which, I would stress, is subject to revision, a summary based on the evidence, as it appears now, presented by over-paintings and various art-styles.

PERIOD OF THE ROUND-HEADED MEN

Ancient Phase
It seems that the most ancient paintings are those of small human figures with schematic bodies and round heads, all painted in violaceous ochre. The heads, moreover, were always exaggeratedly large. Sometimes the top of the head is bare, but often it bears horns or a pendant object which appears to represent feathers. The clothing (which is not represented on all the figures) is just a scanty loin-cloth with two or three ends hanging down. The arms are variously depicted, but often, indeed generally, they are reduced to mere sticks. There are also to be noted in these paintings

bows and a sort of lance or pitchfork about half as high again as a man. There is no 'scene' which can be interpreted as such, and animals are uncommon—when they do occur, mostly elephant and mouflon.

This very peculiar human type, with round head and loin-cloth with pendant ends, is a basic element in the Tassili prehistoric paintings for its standards are to be recognized in the later artistic phases. Red may replace violaceous ochre, the bodies may become filiform or thread-like, but the head remains the same. At least five later phases are derived from this early one, and they do not much differ from it except by an improvement in technique and by the introduction of more animated drawing, especially noticeable in dance scenes with horned men looking like little devils. We may note that all these paintings are in pigment of one colour except for the little devils of the 'advanced' phase, where yellow ochre is found as well as violaceous.

Evolved Phase
The appearance of polychrome paintings marks the beginning of this phase. The style is still that of the 'Round-Heads', but the figures are of larger size and are better treated. The limbs are no longer just 'sticks', but are 'podgy'; they have some thickness. However, arms and forearms, thighs and legs are not clearly defined. Fingers and toes are not separately represented. The women's breasts—always very small—are placed together one above the other on a perpendicular plane. It is true that we also found some monochrome paintings which must be assigned to this phase (such as the white ladies in the Negro mask fresco at Aouanrhet), but most of the pictures are executed in yellow, greenish-yellow or light-red ochre with an outline of dark-red ochre.

This art-phase, like the preceding one, consists of several sub-phases which can, from certain technical or decorative details,

N

easily be recognized. The artists had come to take more and more care in the representation of their subjects, which include not only human figures but also those of elephant, rhinoceros, *Hippocervidae* and mouflon. The head of the men stands out less than in the preceding stages and within the circle of its outline appear strange motifs—parallel lines, triangles, half-circles. Then the artistic quality improves further, forms become more graceful and great attention is paid to details. Bracelets or anklets can be indentified and there are belts, hair or shoulder ornaments (e.g. feather head-dresses), markings (very numerous) on the breasts, belly, thighs, legs or arms, and these may be interpreted either as scarifications or painted designs. The marks, indeed, which are made up of regular rows of dots, recall, very forcibly, those still to be seen among the populations of the Upper Nile or of Central Africa. These markings confirm the undoubtedly 'negroid' character of the paintings and prove, moreover, that in prehistoric times Black Africa stretched much farther north than it does now. This evidence is valuable and new, especially as we still know nothing as to the origin of the Negroes or about the period when they occupied the African continent.

Special Styles

At the end of the foregoing period and at a date which cannot be fixed precisely yet, there was an obvious Egyptian influence in the Tassili and this influence is clear in several works of an exceptionally high quality. The new art-tradition mingled with that of the 'negroid' substratum and gave rise to three categories of quite original paintings.

First of all, there is at Aouanrhet a human figure with bandy legs and wearing a Negro mask. The body is painted in red ochre and is covered with delicate crisscross in white. From both arms and thighs rise stylized flowers. The mask (which in its conventionalization is typical of West Africa today) resembles one still in use among the Sienuf populations of the Ivory Coast where it is employed in initiation ceremonies. The occurrence of such a figure in the heart of the Sahara is, then, of great importance. We know now for the first time, thanks to this Aouanrhet painting, that initiation masks of an animistic character were used in prehistoric ages.

Then come the strange compositions of which the most typical specimen is that of the 'swimming woman'—also at Aouanrhet—a woman with her limbs stretched out and with breasts on her back. She seems to be pulling along through the water a man she holds by the head. He is represented in the 'foetal' position.[1] Below, another man is emerging from an ovoid object, marked with concentric circles and suggesting either an egg or, less probably, a snail's shell. One must be prudent in attempting any interpretation of this scene, since it presents a pictorial theme that is quite unique. What we can say is that these figures are found in an art-phase where Egyptian influences are marked. If we take into account beliefs current in dynastic Egypt—beliefs which must have had their origins in predynastic times, it may be this picture represents the voyage of the dead in the Other World.

Outstanding also is the group of figures of which our 'Antinea' is the most remarkable. This magnificent painting was found in a low-roofed shelter where the picture is difficult to view. It is, indeed, curious that a work of such high quality should not have been put in a more prominent place. We may note that the fringe hanging over the hand links this painting, from an ethnological point of view, with the 'White Lady' of Aouanrhet. At other Jabbaren sites we found male figures in the same style; unfortunately, however, these were very effaced, but the peculiar head-dress of the men—a sort of helmet composed of multi-coloured strips and set below a round cap—can be noticed. Later on we were lucky

[1] That is to say with knees drawn up against the chest as a foetus in the womb.

enough to discover at Sefar two further human figures in the same style and fairly well preserved. Then there were three stylized masks, executed in the same colours, which show this head-dress as seen from the front. These pictures, so unlike in their feeling, although contemporary, wherein are to be seen side by side very naturalistic figures and stylized masks, present a problem which, it would seem, can be solved only if we assume the co-existence of a number of different ethnical groups. The woman, with her straight nose, indicates a Mediterranean influence, although some Egyptian features can be noticed. The 'Greek warriors' of Sefar, although their noses are thicker, appear, too as aliens in Africa.The stylization of the three masks is, however, typically that of negroids. Thus we have a Negro-Egyptian complex which may be explained by the presence, side by side, of men some of whom had been subjected to Egyptian traditions and others to those of negroids. This theory seems plausible enough if we take into account the great variety of the Tassili paintings.

Furthermore, we again find Egyptian influence in a whole series of human figures at Jabbaren and Sefar, figures which are easily recognizable by their head-dress and by the very peculiar treatment for which were utilized a bluish-grey, a very red ochre and a white pigment.

Geology and Painting
One is, first of all, surprised at the multitude of tints to be observed in the Tassili paintings, for such an abundance of different colours was unusual in prehistoric art, since the painters employed, generally speaking, a simplified palette consisting mostly of red ochre, a kaolin white and oxide of manganese. However, in the Tassili, there exist schists which occur, as outcrops, for miles on end, and we found these in abundance on the plateau between the Tamrit and Jabbaren massifs. These ochreous schists are, in part, retilted,

73. *Iherir: The Kayak on a Gelta*

74. *Tuareg Family living in a Rock-Shelter*

75. Prehistoric Millstone and Pounders

76. Neolithic Flint Arrow-Heads

and emerge, to a greater or lesser extent, from the ground, so that from one stratum to another they have been subjected to a greater or lesser intense action of the sun's rays. The consequence of this has been that the colours of these schists have been changed in various ways. The deposits which were the most protected are of a very dark ochre colour—almost chocolate—then the range of tints comprises brick-red, light red and yellow—this latter presenting a whole variety of shades, ending up with a markedly greenish tone.

These ochres, when ground to powder, must have been mixed with media whose exact nature is not certain but which included —if we base our supposition on analyses made of remains of paintings from Jebel Uwenat[1]—both casein (from milk) and acacia gum. We noticed, too, that the consistency of the ochres was not the same in all epochs. Thus, the paintings of the 'Round Head' style in yellow ochre show coatings of paint which originally must have been quite thick. Again, the subjects of the 'Bovidian' phase were executed with a more fluid pigment which penetrated deeper into the surface of the rock.

Decadent Style

What seems to be the final phase of the 'Round Head' style (but which I should not, in the present state of our knowledge, venture to date absolutely either before or after these three very individual and peculiar styles, though I think the final phase comes before them) is, compared with the other and preceding art-phases, obviously decadent from the aesthetic point of view. The drawing is coarser, the forms are heavy and there are no carefully executed details. The technique itself is simple to a degree—the figures are reduced to a red-ochre outline (often doubled with yellow ochre)

[1] The Jebel Uwenat is a mountainous mass on the borders of Libya and southern Egypt; the site presents a number of prehistoric paintings.

and the bodies are filled in with white. Gigantic size is the characteristic of this phase and one gets the impression that the artists were more concerned with making their pictures imposing than beautiful.

For instance, we found on one wall—where it reached from the ground to the roof—a human figure measuring about fifteen feet in height but which, if we take into account the lower part, now much effaced, must originally have been over eighteen feet tall. It is, perhaps, unnecessary to mention that never before had there been discovered rupestral paintings of this size. Moreover, the figure in question holds the record as being the largest prehistoric painting in the world. Other figures, in the same style, and found at Sefar measure, as much as eleven feet and must, without doubt, represent divinities of the prehistoric Tassilians. In addition to the human figures, this archaeological phase (very abundantly represented in the eastern Tassili) includes numerous animals which give us a good idea of the variety of the fauna then existing in the Sahara: elephants, giraffes, wild oxen, *Hippocervidae*, mouflon, warthogs, lions (one of the feline paintings is over twelve feet long), ostriches. Certain of these animals may, perhaps, have played a magic role for they are often found in association with women whose arms are raised in an attitude of adoration or supplication. Sometimes the composite forms of certain animals remind one of the monsters of classical mythology, but they are creatures to which no name can be put.

With this 'decadent' phase the great period of the 'Round Head' paintings closes.

From a time that was, no doubt, but little posterior to that of the execution of the 'White Lady' of Aouanrhet foreign influences began to be felt and these may be evidence for the first migrations which announced the 'Bovidian' invasion. But however this may be, the art of the negroid peoples—already several thousands of

years old—was on the decline. Soon the Tassili was invaded by
newcomers who in no way resembled their predecessors and who
pushed before them into the upper valleys herds of slow-moving
cattle. Thenceforth the walls of the Tassili shelters were to be
covered with pictures of an absolutely new style and in an entirely
new tradition.

THE 'BOVIDIAN' PERIOD

These new-style paintings consist of human and animal figures
of small size treated in an admirably naturalistic way. When we
look on the enthralling assemblages of the 'Bovidian' period we
must, I think, conclude that they represent the greatest naturalistic
school in the world. Here is no more semi-schematization, no
more stylization, no more symbolism as in the previous art-phases
of the Tassili. We have living creatures caught in movement,
seized by the artist as they exhibited their most lively attitudes and
reproduced with a fidelity and a vigour which attest to an incomparable acuity of observation. The 'Bovidians' employed
principally red ochre, but they also used yellow ochre and white
pigment, these two latter in order to render animals' hair, to
bring out certain details and sometimes to trace an outline.

Cattle are the favourite subject of these artists. It is clear from
the number of the oxen and from the artistic quality of their
representations that these beasts occupied a place of great importance in men's lives. They are fine creatures with lithe and
active bodies kept fit and trim by grazing about over the savanna-
like steppes. There are no signs of the masses of fat induced by a
sedentary life in enclosed pastures too rich in green plants. The
cattle have long horns either in the form of a lyre or in that of a
semicircle, and the horns seem to indicate the presence of two
different species, well known in dynastic Egypt, the African ox or

Bos africanus and the *Bos brachyceros* or thick-horned ox. The representations of these animals are presented either in flat tints or in outlines, and the beasts themselves are generally shown in large herds followed by their herdsmen. A picture I discovered at Tamrit during my first stay in the Tassili was composed of no less than sixty-five beasts—it remains the largest assemblage of any known to this day. Another painting at Jabbaren, although it has fewer animals, is of a still finer artistic quality both from the point of view of the composition and also from that of the beauty and harmony of the colours which include, as an exception, yellow, green, violaceous and even blue tints such as have never been seen in any other prehistoric painting and which suggest a knowledge of new pigments or anyway of new combinations of colours such as were, no doubt, reserved for a few special artists.

The wild animals are treated no less skilfully and the 'Bovidian' pastoralists, who were also hunters, left for us a whole menagerie which gives a clear and accurate picture of the tropical fauna which formerly inhabited the Sahara—elephants, rhinoceroses. hippopotamuses, giraffes, *Hippocervidae*, gazelles, aard-varks, lions, wild asses, ostriches, fish and unidentified equines. Such an abundance of wild life implies the existence of a very damp climate and rich pastures which is further proved by a fresco at Aouanrhet depicting three hippopotamuses being chased by men in a canoe.

Both beasts and men are shown grouped as in life. You see human figures in the midst of an oval that seems to represent the ground-plan of an oblong hut whose door (which is sometimes shown) indicates clearly the materials used for its construction—straw or esparto. In fact, just the same sort of hut made of vegetable matter and standing on a foundation of pottery as is to be found today in all the French Sudan. In other paintings you can see women standing before their cooking-pots, men with axes in their hands and ready to split wood, children lying under a

coverlet, people sitting in a circle and conversing, couples con-
joined in the act of procreation and many other scenes which
reveal what was the material life of these pastoralists who, moreover, must already have practised some sort of agriculture as is
indicated by a group of women tilling a field.

Warlike activities (occasioned as the frescoes indicate by theft
and need to protect flocks and herds) seem to have been considerable and the pictures which illustrate them are of extraordinary realism. The paintings are so vividly expressive that,
despite the small size of the figures, it is possible to read in the faces
the various emotions felt by the combatants. These scenes of
struggle are equalled only by the dance pictures which are admirably composed. You can see women executing graceful bounds
in the air while others clap their hands to keep time and still
others shake little instruments like rattles.

Although, on the whole, the work of the 'Bovidian' artists was
on a small scale they did also sometimes execute figures almost
life-size and these are often works of very exceptional quality.
At Tin Abou Teka we saw two archers five feet three inches high
and most admirably painted. At Jabbaren there was a group of
women whose head-dresses, like crested helmets or sugar-loaves,
recall those of the Peul women in West Africa. All these large
paintings, and especially the one we called 'Man and Woman
Seated', are astonishingly beautiful. In no other part of the world
did prehistoric artists treat the human body with such skill—we
have, indeed, to wait for the Greeks before we find comparable
works of art.

The animals also, in some cases, are executed on a large scale,
as, for instance, several oxen, a feline, and an aard-vark which we
saw at Jabbaren and Tin Abou Teka. The origin of these herdsmen
would have been mysterious enough had we not discovered
decisive evidence that they came from the Upper Nile. Indeed,

in six different sites we found 'Bovidian' pictures in which were representations of typical Egyptian boats with the standards of the nomes[1] at the prow. The really extraordinary fact that such characteristic paintings exist on the Tassili rocks proves that these pastoralists had had, at one time, contacts with the Valley of the Nile and that, in all probability, the 'Bovidians' came from the east.

Such, then, as I see it from my first attempts at interpretation, are the main art-phases which can be distinguished in the Tassili frescoes. It must be admitted that there are other pictures, such as certain semi-schematized human figures painted in white, those of the elongated 'filiform' men of Jabbaren and those of little archers in Spanish[2] style at Timenzouzine; and there are still others, but I have not, as yet, the information necessary to situate these chronologically and I mention them just to make my catalogue complete.

Certain hunters, for instance, their bodies covered with paint and shown, sometimes, with javelins in their hands and at other times armed with axes, are treated in a quite special way. Sometimes, also, there are outline figures which show grotesque and often amusing profiles. We called this latter style the 'Humoristic'.

There are also to be seen hand stencils which resemble those in the prehistoric grottoes of palaeolithic Europe. At Ti-n-Tazarift we found some of these 'hands' placed over 'Bovidian' paintings which indicates that such stencils are posterior to, or possibly contemporary with, the 'Bovidian' epoch.

One of the most unexpected of our discoveries was that of two typically Egyptian style paintings at Jabbaren. The first shows four tutelary goddesses with birds' heads. This scene is one of

[1] The 'nomes' were the ancient provinces of dynastic (and also it would seem, of predynastic) Egypt, each one of which had its own standard, e.g. the hawk.
[2] 'Spanish', that is to say, Levantine (i.e. eastern) Spanish prehistoric rock-paintings, are probably more recent than those of the Franco-Cantabrian complex.

offerings. They are the only examples of their kind that we came across and they present a puzzling problem, for no one, up to now, has suggested that the Egyptians penetrated as far to the west of the Nile as the Tassili. Perhaps these pictures are just the work of some Egyptianized Libyan or of some Egyptian prisoners carried off by the Libyans to their country. I would hasten, however, to add that these suggestions are quite gratuitous since it is impossible to draw valid conclusions from such scanty evidence.

'Horse' and 'Camel' period pictures, which fall into historical times and are well represented on some Saharan sites, were, comparatively speaking, not numerous in the region we prospected. We did, however, come across a few pictures of chariots. I have referred to these before and have stressed the interest they present.

As well as copying the paintings we sought also for traces which the astonishing populations of artists may have left near their works. We were able to find a considerable number of grinding-stones and mullers while in certain shelters bits of pottery literally covered the ground. I did some digging at the foot of painted rock-walls and in several places found abundant remains of meals mixed with objects identical with those on the surface, not only the same grinding-stones and mullers and the same pottery, but also stone axes, flint arrow-heads, scrapers and remains of ornaments such as necklace beads cut out of ostrich egg-shell and schist pendants and bracelets.

All these objects had been abandoned, it seems, by the 'Bovidian' populations. Charcoal was recovered from among the ashes, and when it has been submitted to the carbon-14 test[1] we shall have a

---

[1] The carbon-14 test, by which can be determined the age of any object of organic origin (by counting the amount of radio-carbon present, since this diminishes at a regular rate after the death of the organism), is now valid for a period of up to 70,000 years. However, the test must not be regarded as in all cases absolutely reliable, since there is always a risk of contamination.

good idea as to the date of the 'Bovidian' paintings. Provisionally, however, they can be assigned to about 3500 B.C. That would be a rough dating for the arrival of the pastoralists, but they must have sojourned long in the Sahara—maybe several thousand years.

The other pictures belonging to the various phases of the 'Round Heads' type of art are much more ancient. The very first stages must be assigned to a Neolithic without grinding-stones or pottery and whose principal implements were coarsely chipped stone axes. If one dates these paintings to about eight thousand years ago (and thus to the very early Neolithic), I think we shall be within the bounds of reason.

Perhaps in this short summary I have indicated the considerable amount of new information that the Tassili rock-paintings add to our knowledge of the Sahara's past. Of course, since the close study of our documentary evidence has hardly yet begun, what I have done here is to present somewhat fragmentary data as I collected it on the spot—data which, however, careful and precise laboratory work will, we hope, make more illuminating in the future.

77 to 88. The Main Art Styles

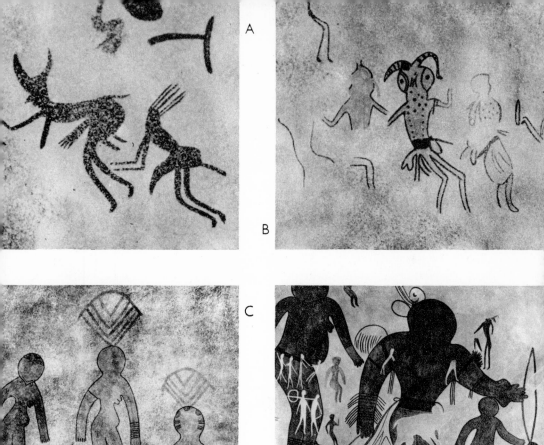

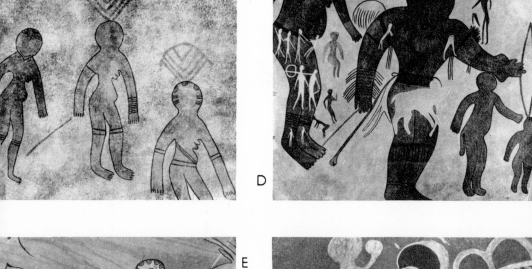

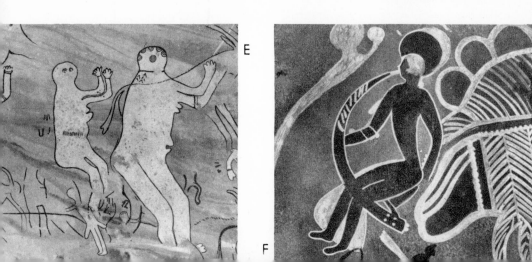

G

H

I

J

K

L

The Main Art Styles

The plates give an idea of the different art-phases to be distinguished in the Tassili paintings. The table, of course, presents only a schematic, incomplete and provisional view. As we collected such abundant material much work will have to be done in checking the data before, after a complete inventory has been made, a final balance can be struck.

A *Style of Small Round-Headed Figures with Horns.*
Horned and plumed individuals belonging to what are considered as the most ancient phases.

B *Style of the 'Little Devils'.*
Evolved style of representation. The influence of the 'Martian' phase with 'Round-Headed' men can be perceived. In yellow ochre with red-ochre outline.

C *Style of the 'Round-Headed Men' (Middle Period).*
'Martian' phase. Yellow ochre with red-ochre outlines.

D *Style of the 'Round-Headed Men' (Evolved Phase).*
Evolved 'Martian' style (as far as the individual in the middle is concerned; for the others *see* above, No. 22).

E   *Style of the 'Round-Headed Men' (Decadent Phase).*
Decadent 'Martian' style. More lavish use of white pigment
with yellow-ochre outlines.

F   *Style of the 'Round-Headed Men' (Egyptian Influence).*
Final period (phase of the 'White Lady' of Aouanrhet).

G   *Style of the Hunters with Painted Bodies (Ancient Bovidian Phase).*

H   *Bovidian Style.*
Classical style. Individual of Hamitic type.

I   *Style of the 'Judges' (Post-Bovidian Epoch).*
Figures of the 'Judges' and 'Antinea' type. Egyptian influence.

J   *Style of the Elongated 'White Men' of Post-Bovidian Date.*
Figures in linear style. It is certain that they are Post-Bovidian
but it is not clear whether or not they are posterior to the
'Judges' phase.

K   *Style of the Chariot Period.*
Type of the 'Flying Gallop'.

L   *Style of the 'Bi-Triangular' Men. Period of Mounted Horses.*

Notes on the Illustrations

In the middle of the fresco a large figure 3.25 metres high. On the left, women raising their arms in supplication. On the right, painted over an antelope in dark red and the white horns of another antelope above, is a woman lying on her back. Her position and her swollen abdomen suggest that she is about to give birth. The scene is no doubt a magic one and is connected with some fertility cult. The most ancient portion of the painting is a large white horn—to the left of the central figure. Traces, which cannot be seen on the copy, show that this horn is one of a pair, probably belonging to a specimen of *Bubalus antiquus*. This representation is the only one of its sort that we found in the Tassili. There can also be seen in this painting some small human figures with round heads (belonging to the ancient epoch) and to the right seated figures (of the 'Bovidian' epoch).

Fragment. See note on No. 28 below.

PLATES IN BLACK AND WHITE

1 *In the Sefar Massif.*
The Tassili sandstones within the Sefar massif. Here they are
relatively compact and are not more than from 25 to 30 metres
high. Note the superficial erosion due to water-action and the
hollows at the base—which are very common.

2 *On the Track from Sefar to Tamrit.*
The 'Fairy Funnels' of the Oued Iddo.

3 *The Expedition's Guides and Tuareg.*
A short halt during which the native personnel quickly makes
tea. In the foreground, dry *shebrok* branches collected to feed
the fire.

3a LINE DRAWING. *Two Sketches of Frescoes.*

4 *The Tafalelet Pass.*
The track from Djanet to Ghat goes through the Tafalelet
Pass leading up to the Tassili. The ascent is one of the steepest
and most difficult to negotiate. In the photograph the per-
spective is distorted but there is more than four hundred
and fifty feet difference in altitude between the top and the
spur of rock to be seen in the background to the right. Masses
of stone are piled up in the passage and there is often hardly
room to get a pack animal through the rubble. The members
of the expedition went up and down this pass more than
fifty times either to carry supplies or to take the mail to Djanet.

5 *Camp-fire at Sefar*
Every evening the members of the mission, both French and
Tuareg, gathered round the camp-fire. This was the time of

day for rest when stories were told or the day's work com-
mented on or the next day's programme discussed. The
setting and the lighting of these gatherings lent them a definitely 'prehistoric' appearance. This photograph was taken
at Sefar during the second part of the expedition.

6 *Sefar. Swabbing Down a Rock-face.*
When we had discovered a painting on a wall it was carefully
washed down by means of a soft sponge. This treatment
allowed us not only to revive the colours, but also to distinguish more clearly the picture itself. Here can be seen the
'Headless Man' of Sefar.

7 *I-n-Tifnar. Taking a Tracing.*
The paintings were traced on the rock-surface by means of
very tough and very clear transparent paper. The operation,
which sounds simple enough, was, in fact, often a very ticklish
matter. Sometimes the painting itself was not very distinct,
sometimes the wind shifted and tore the paper, sometimes
the whole thing was hampered by the uncomfortable position
in which we had to work. The tracing was always corrected
later on so as to rectify any possible distortion due to the rock-
surface and to fill in delicate details which our pencils, because
of the granular texture of the wall, had not been able to
reproduce.

8 *Sefar. Transfer of Tracing onto Drawing-paper.*
The sheet of drawing-paper on to which the picture was to be
reproduced was, first of all, covered with a coating of *gouache*
in the same tint as that of the rock. Then the tracing was
transferred, by means of special pencils. Finally the copy was
checked off with the original painting. In this photograph can
o

be seen the frescoes covering the wall of the Amazons' shelter at Sefar. Note the small human figures and the flock of sheep.

9 *Sefar. Colouring of a Copy in the Headless Man Shelter.*
When the tracing had been transferred to the drawing-paper, colour was applied in *gouache* by our artists in front of the originals. Since all the work was done on the spot absolutely faithful reproductions were obtained that offer the greatest possible degree of authenticity. The colours used were those of the paintings after they had been freshened up by application of water and so restored to their original brightness. In this photograph one of the expedition's artists is working in the 'Headless Man' shelter at Sefar.

10 *Painted Rock-Shelter at Aouanrhet.*
One type of shelter. There were many, differing both in their shape and size. Some were not more than three feet long and broad, whereas others were as much as 300 feet long. At Jabbaren and Aouanrhet the rocks often were in the form of beehives or Negroes' huts. The hollow here shown displayed the running figures (vide No. 38) as well as other subjects which we were not able to copy.

11 *The Great Shelter at Jabbaren.*
Another type of painted shelter, at Jabbaren. It is about 180 feet long and almost its whole length is covered with pictures. The depth varies from ten to twenty feet. In some places there are, on the ground, vestiges of an archaeological deposit containing remains of meals—animal bones, ash, charcoal, as well as fragments of pottery and necklace beads cut out of ostrich egg-shell. Run-off waters had, however, destroyed most of the deposit and had washed many objects out of the

shelter and scattered them on the ground outside where they may be found on the surface.

12 *Tamrit. The Fresco of the Hunters (detail). Bovidian Period.*
    (42 × 25 cm.)
    A portion of the great hunters' fresco at Tamrit discovered by Henri Lhote in 1934. The painting is situated in a shelter which may well be called a cave, since it is more than eighteen feet deep and is, because of this depth, rather dark. The grotto also contains other paintings belonging to the 'Round Headed Men' phase and among which is a large mouflon. The hunters have painted designs on their bodies and are armed either with bows or javelins. The game is represented only by heads which suggest those of sheep, but such an identification is not certain, especially as the blotches indicating the fur or hair do not much resemble the wool of sheep. The painting offers one technical peculiarity: the outlines were made with light strokes before the surfaces were coloured. The fresco must belong to the 'ancient Bovidian' period. The colours used are red and yellow ochre and white. The work is one of great delicacy and is remarkable both for its composition and the quality of the execution.

13 *Upper Tamrit. The 'Egyptian' Boat. Bovidian Period.*
    (103 × 76 cm.)
    This fresco is painted on the roof of a very low shelter into which we had to crawl. Inside, a man can hardly sit, much less stand. There are two motifs of the same sort and, at first, we took them for pictures of snakes. However, other discoveries made at Jabbaren and at Ti-n-Tazarift enabled me to identify the objects as Nile boats such as are to be seen represented on the rocks of Upper Egypt. These engravings are

considered to be of pre-dynastic date (i.e. earlier than about 3000 B.C.). *See* H. A. Winkler. *Rock-Drawings of Southern Egypt.* London, 1938, Vol. I. Plates xxxiii to xl. The Tamrit pictures of boats may be assigned to the pastoralists' period and prove that the 'Bovidians' had been in contact with Upper Egypt, whence, in all probability, they came.

14 *Tamrit. The Two Venuses. Bovidian Period.*
    (30 × 57 cm.)
    A small fresco at Tamrit (detail). It was found on the rock-face of a cliff in a valley parallel to that of the Oued Tamrit and communicating with the latter by a passage situated about eighty yards downstream from the 'Hunters' Shelter' (No. 12). These Venuses, treated in a style recalling that of Maillol, are painted in red ochre, and reveal a perfect knowledge of the human frame. The ox, which has been added later, is an outline drawing (Bovidian Period).

15 *Upper Tamrit. The* Sable *Antelopes. Bovidian Period.*
    (100 × 137 cm.)
    This fresco is painted on the perpendicular wall of a small shelter overlooking the upper reaches of the *wadi*, near a *tarout* tree that grows among the rocks and not far from a little *geltah*. The subjects are antelopes of the sable, roan or addax kind. Red ochre and white. A masterpiece of the Bovidian phase. Below, the gazelle in yellow ochre has been shifted slightly upwards in our reproduction.

16 *Jebrin, the Expedition's Guide.*
    Our guide, Jebrin-ag-Mohammed, about sixty-five years old. He belongs to the *Imrad* tribe of the Kel Medak. The best guide

in the Tassili. Quite exceptional for a Tuareg, he is red-haired and has blue eyes; his body is covered with freckles.

17 *Tamrit. The Stripped Tarout. The man to be seen in the photograph is the guide Sermi.*
One of the Tamrit cypresses (*Cupressus dupreziana*). A Tuareg is cutting one of the upper branches. The tree had some time before had its head lopped off and was, most probably, condemned to die in a short while.

18 *Timenzouzine. Human Figures with Body Paintings. Bovidian Period.*
(55 × 70 cm.)
Fresco in the large shelter at Timenzouzine (detail). These figures with painted bodies recall those of the Tamrit hunters. The former, however, are of coarser execution. They hold in their hands instruments whose shape resembles that of neolithic axes. The pendant object that hangs down between the legs of the figure at the top is certainly not a penis sheath but the end of a loin-cloth. Below, from left to right, a hippopotamus head, three giraffes and a wild buffalo. The animal above seems to be equine. The whole assemblage is Bovidian.

19 *Timenzouzine. Elephant Engraved on a Stone Rock.* Bubalus *Period.*
(236 × 219 cm.)
Situated on the right bank of the Oued Timenzouzine. The engraving has been filled in with chalk so as to make its outline more visible on the photograph. The picture belongs to the *Bubalus* Period and is thus very ancient, perhaps more ancient than any others of the paintings we discovered. There were very few engravings in the area we prospected. Here is a list of them: a human figure (in addition to the elephant) at Timenzouzine, a group of short-tailed sheep near the Oued

Amazzar, an ithyphallic human figure at Ouan Abou, a rhinoceros near Oua-Moulin and an unidentifiable subject at Jabbaren; that was all. It has already been suggested that the engravings and paintings, far from being the work of one people, were probably executed by different populations. This, at least, would seem to be true for the Bovidian and Pre-Bovidian Periods. In this connection, the absence, in the region which we were able to explore methodically, of any engravings representing cattle, would seem to be significant.

20 *Jabbaren. Antelope with an Elephant's Body. Decadent Period of the 'Round Heads'.*
(105 × 130 cm.)
Outline painting in red ochre doubled with white. It is situated, not in a shelter, but in a rock-hollow overlooking the Oued Jabbaren (left bank). The picture belongs to the 'Round Head' Period of which the 'Great Martian God' is typical.

21 *Jabbaren. The 'Great Martian God.' Decadent Period of the 'Round Heads'.*
(Reduced in scale to 93 × 130 cm.)
The Great 'Martian' God of Jabbaren. It occupies all the wall of the 'great shelter' on the left bank of the *wadi*. This wall is markedly concave and since the head is painted on the roof the whole is very difficult to see. We camped, in fact, nearly a fortnight near the picture without noticing it. Yet this enormous figure, if we take into account the lower part which is effaced, must be nearly eighteen feet in height. Numerous paintings which can be referred to this art-phase are to be seen not only at Jabbaren, but also at Adjefou, at Ti-n-Tazarift and at Sefar. They are of great size and all are executed in the same style: white body with a red

outline which is sometimes doubled by a yellow outline. Beside these figures there occur (*see* No. 20) elephants, antelopes, warthogs, giraffes, mouflon, ostriches, lions and fantastic animal shapes.

22 *Jabbaren. Archer with Plumed Head-dress. 'Round Heads' Period (Evolved).*
(100 × 105 cm.)
The fresco is in the 'Mess Corridor' at Jabbaren. The painting, of which a part only is shown here, was completely hidden under a layer of clayey dust which adhered very firmly to the rock-face. It took half a day to wash the wall and to reveal the picture. There are several art-phases represented: (1) The three little human figures one above the other which are visible between the large figures of a man and a woman and which are executed in a violaceous red ochre. (2) The four large figures in brick-red ochre with outlines and body decorations in dark ochre. They belong to the 'Martian' type. Note, on the woman's body, dotted designs which probably represent scarifications. The man holds a short plain curved bow. This group of paintings is older than the 'Great Martian God,' whose white surface is outlined in red. (3) The elephant over-painted on the man holding the bow is treated in yellow ochre outlined in white. (4) The small bowed figure above the woman's feet is in red ochre and belongs to the 'Bovidian' period. (5) Other small human figures stand out in white.

23 *Jabbaren. The 'Little Devils'. 'Round Heads' Period (Evolved).*
(100 × 67 cm.)
The 'little devils' of Jabbaren. Painting on the wall of an isolated rock (left bank of the *wadi*). These small horned figures, wearing loin-cloths with a number of flaps, are dancers, as may be seen from the cymbals held at arm's length. The style of the

'devils' is derived from that of little figures, with horned round heads, belonging to an ancient art-phase, but the former have been influenced by a later tradition, that of the round-headed figures, of moderate size, generally executed in yellow ochre outlined in white. The 'devils' are themselves painted in violaceous red and in yellow ochre. The rest of the figures, although somewhat differently treated, are, apparently, of the same period.

24 *Jabbaren. Fresco of the Little Archers. 'Round Heads' Period (Evolved).*
(62 × 85 cm.)
Little round-headed figures from upper Jabbaren, painted in violaceous ochre. Some have loin-cloths of triangular shape with decoration in the form of a cross, others are, apparently, naked, but all belong to the same art-phase. The cross design might suggest a knife, but this is certainly not the right interpretation. Rather the design represents some accessory of the loin-cloth. The figures are armed with moderate-sized bows with triple curves.

25 *Jabbaren. Filiform Dancers. Uncertain Period.*
(112 × 40 cm.)
The dancers are painted in pale red ochre and are to be seen on the wall of a cliff rising from the Oued Jabbaren, that is to say, in a spot that can never have been inhabited. The figures are the only ones of their kind we found and the absence of any over-painting prevents us from placing them chronologically.

26 *Jabbaren. Scene of Offerings. Egyptian Influence (18th Dynasty?)*
(105 × 38 cm.)
The fresco was found on the wall of a cliff on the western side

89. Henri Lhote, Head of the Expedition
90 to 101. The Team

Irène Montandon   Claude Guichard

Georges Le Poitevin   Gianni Frassati

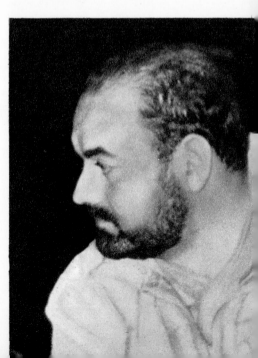

Jacques Violet   Philippe Letellier

Robert Martin   Jack Chambrin

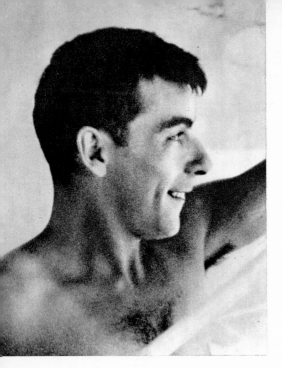

Jean-Dominique Lajoux   *Michel Brézillon*

Jean Lesage   *André Vila*

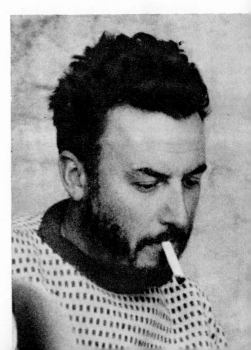

of the *wadi* and not in a shelter. The colours, which are faded, could not be copied before the swabbing down of the rock. The style seems to be derived from that of Egypt but from an Egyptian art tradition that was more free than that of the monuments. All the figures, men and women, have birds' heads and wear Egyptian head-dresses (*pshent?*). The women have skirts and the men loin-cloths—also of Egyptian style. There can also be seen conical vases similar to those of pre-dynastic Egyptian times, and, especially, a ritual boat like those known in Upper Egypt with the standard of the nomes and streamers.

27 *Jabbaren. Engraved Cattle. Bovidian Period.*
(24 × 30 cm.)
This is not, strictly speaking, an engraving but a sketch for a painting, since, before they painted, the 'Bovidians' drew on the rock an outline of the picture. The lines, although very lightly incised, are still observable in many of the finished paintings. It was only at Jabbaren and Adjefou that we found such sketches.

28 *Jabbaren. Polychrome Cattle. Bovidian Period.*
(305 × 105 cm.)
This remarkable fresco in Upper Jabbaren was painted on a rock-face away from any shelter. The oxen belong to two species, one with delicate horns more or less curved into the shape of a lyre—which must represent the *Bos africanus*—and another with thick horns (in this painting represented as projecting forwards) which would be the *Bos brachyceros*. Behind the mass of the marching beasts is a herdsman. In the foreground an animal which has been killed and one of whose legs has already been cut off.

29 *Jabbaren. Cattle and Human Figures (engraved). Bovidian Period.*
(24 × 30 cm.)
Sketch for painting (*see* No. 27).

30 *Jabbaren. The 'Judges'. 'Post-Bovidian' Period with Egyptian Influence.*
(130 × 92 cm.)
The 'Magistrates'. A fresco found under overhanging rock
which, however, did not form a shelter. It was the head-
dresses that induced us to give these figures the name of the
'Judges', which, moreover, do not consist solely of men. It is,
nevertheless, the male figures which wear the curious head-
dresses which are composed of a sort of high cap or toque
(like that of French judges) marked with vertical strips of
different colours upon which is placed a rounded hat in some
cases provided with flaps. The vertical strips are painted in red
and greyish-blue ochre with outlines in white. These men also
wear ornaments on their arms and shoulders. The colour of
the bodies is greyish-blue and the belts are of red ochre with
white outlines. The floral motif to be seen before the persons
in the upper row is in the same white pigment and was doubt-
less painted at the same time as the figures. This motif is
painted over a large feline in red ochre, of which only the
hind-part is shown and which must be dated to the Bovidian
Period. The 'Judges' are 'post-Bovidian' and of the same
period as 'Antinea' (No. 33), the 'Runners' of Aouanrhet
(No. 38) and the stylized Negro masks (No. 53) and the human
figure in No. 51.

31 *Jabbaren. Archer from the Great Hunting Scene. Bovidian Period.*
(20 × 18 cm.)
The archer wears a little white-striped close-fitting cap and a
square-shaped loin-cloth. The moderately sized bow is semi-
circular. Note that the bow is not held in the same manner

as that in No. 24. This latter shows the method of the steppe populations, whereas in this hunting scene the bow is held as is usual among forest-dwelling peoples.

32 *Jabbaren. The Small-headed Woman. Bovidian Period.*
(70 × 75 cm.)
This painting of a woman with a head-dress in the form of a crest was found on the wall we called that of the 'Little Rabbits', and very near the ground. The body, painted in red ochre, is bulky, and the neck and head, by comparison, are very small. The 'crest' of the head-dress seems to be flattened, as is that of Peul women when they remove the stiff framework that serves to support their hair. The dots and blobs in whitish pigment, which are disposed all over the body, are certainly not merely decorative. Most probably they indicate the traces of some sickness such as smallpox. Note that the profile is not of negroid type. The nose is pointed, the lips moderately full, the chin well marked. On the other hand, the forehead is rounded and very high. All these features can be found today among the Peuls.

33 *Jabbaren. 'Antinea'. Post-Bovidian Period with Egyptian Influence.*
(115 × 185 cm.)
This magnificent female figure was found in the so-called 'Aard-Vark' shelter at Jabbaren where it is situated in the least accessible part of the grotto and screened from outside by a huge rock. The shelter had been occupied (previously to the execution of the painting) by Bovidians, who left here remains of their repasts and a number of artefacts. The great picture covers, to the extreme right, a little round-headed figure, while a Bovidian personage in red ochre seems to have been embodied in the head-dress of 'Antinea'. The profile is typically 'European'—Greek one might almost say. It is in marked

contrast with the coarse faces of the 'magistrates' (No. 30) and of the women of the Upper Jabbaren (List of Styles No. 1) which, nevertheless, belong to the same art-phase and are all executed in similar colours. The head-dress seems to indicate an important personage. Here, once more, we see the head-band or high cap which is characteristic of this school of painting, but the upper part of the head-dress is different and appears to contain an attribute whose form is not unlike that of the Egyptian *pshent*. The hand seems to be covered by a frill or fringe.

34 *Jabbaren. The 'Peul' Girls. Bovidian Period.*
(90 × 130 cm.)
These two fine figures were discovered on the face of the cliff bordering on the left bank of the Oued Jabbaren and distant only a few yards from the 'Oblation Scene' (No. 26) and the 'Little Egyptian Women'. These 'Peul Girls' are in red ochre with head-dress and robes in white. Two of the forearms have been effaced. The profiles are not negroid and recall those of the Peul women today who wear similar head-dresses. The arms and hands are treated much in the style of certain 18th and 20th dynasty Egyptian paintings (see *Les chefs-d'œuvre de la peinture égyptienne*, by André Lhote). Furthermore, the robes are those which the women of the people wore at the same epoch (op. cit. vide plates 28, 29 and 42). The horse over-painted and visible to the left dates from the 'Equine' Period.

35 *Aouanrhet. The Horned Goddess or 'White Lady'. Period of 'Evolved' Round Heads. Egyptian Influence.*
(100 × 150 cm.)
This fresco, one of the most remarkable, for its pictorial quality, of any in the Tassili, was discovered on an isolated

rock whose base is hollowed out into a number of small shelters that could not have been used as dwellings. The picture is in yellow ochre and white. The dots on the body, the shoulders and the breasts most probably represent scarifications. The loin-cloth and the attributes of the dance, armlets and garters, are composed of, or decorated with, a network of fibres or fine thongs as are the wrist-flounces. The ankles are adorned with broad plaits which seem to be of the same material as the flounces over the wrists—probably fibre. The horns of the head appear to hold up a field of wheat from which grains are falling. Perhaps we have here the figure of a priestess of some agricultural religion or the picture of a goddess of such a cult who foreshadows—or is derived from—the goddess Isis, to whom, in Egypt, was attributed the discovery of agriculture. The little bust which can be seen painted below, under an arch, is of the same epoch as the 'White Lady' herself—that is to say, that of the latest phase of the 'Round Heads'. The small figures in red ochre are of Bovidian Period. These seem to have been covered by the 'White Lady' and this impression is especially marked in the loin-cloth and the fringes that hang from the arms. In these places the figures show through, but, as a matter of fact, they were over-painted and the effect of transparence is due to the red ochre of the figures not having adhered to the white and so having disappeared. The little figure in white to the left is 'post-Bovidian'.

36 *Aouanrhet. The Swimming Woman with Breasts on her Back. Post-Bovidian Period with Egyptian Influence.*
(127 × 85 cm.)
This painting was discovered under a beehive rock and in a shelter too small ever to have served as a dwelling. The scene is a complex one. Above, is a woman stretched out and towing

a man whose limbs are doubled up. Below, to the left, a figure, with outstretched arms, is emerging from a curious ovoid object. The colours are white outlined in red ochre (the top-most figure), ochre dotted with white for the head-dresses, as well as a greenish-yellow ochre for the motif below. The two figures situated respectively above the ovoid and below the man in tow, although added later, are of the same epoch as the main subjects, as is also the figure to be seen upright at the bottom of the double page, to the right. On the other hand, the two little figures in red ochre in the middle of the right-hand page are of 'Bovidian' age. I have mentioned (p. 82) how difficult this fresco is to interpret. Have we here a memento of the voyage of the dead and of birth? This is merely a suggestion. The style, however, is clearly comparable with that of the Jabbaren 'Judges' (No. 30). Note especially the resemblance between the head-dresses, the profiles, the arm ornaments and the shape of the breasts. In a certain measure, also, the pigments are the same, red ochre, white, greenish-yellow ochre.

37 *Aouanrhet. The Negro Mask. Period of the 'Round Heads' anterior to that of the 'Decadent Styles'.*
(90 × 130 cm.)
This fresco is in the middle of a deep and rather dark shelter which, in its shape and form, distinctly reminds one of a sanctuary. The tall white woman to the right dates from an early phase of the Round-Headed men period. A second female figure, still partly visible, is covered by the masked man, which is treated in brick-red ochre and the body covered with a white chequer-work pattern. The position of the figure rather resembles that of a man on horseback. Neither hands nor feet are represented. The only article of clothing is a long

loin-cloth of triangular shape held up by a cord. The mask, which is elongated in form and is horned, is of the same shape as certain Negro masks still used in West Africa. For instance, the Sienuf of the Ivory Coast employ an initiation mask of the same type but with the horns turned outwards. Note also the plants (flowers?) which issue from the arms and thighs. This painting is, in date, older than the phase represented by the 'Great Martian God' of Jabbaren.

38 *Aouanrhet. The 'Marathon Race'. Post-Bovidian Period with Egyptian Influence.*
(155 × 60 cm.)
This group of figures, which appear to be running, is painted on the wall of a niche and almost at the level of the ground. The picture is in white, greyish-blue and red ochre, pigments that are typical of the 'Judges' art-phase (*see* No. 30). Furthermore, on a very irregular rock-face were also painted figures like those of the Upper Jabbaren (*see* List of Styles, No. 1). Unfortunately this latter picture was much effaced and could not be copied. Note the head-dresses, different from those of the 'Judges', but which recall certain ancient Egyptian head-bands.

39 *Aouanrhet. The Negress with Tattooed Breasts. Post-Bovidian Period with Egyptian Influence.*
(110 × 95 cm.)
Fresco found in the same shelter as the 'Swimming Woman with Breasts on Her Back' (No. 36). The Negress—to the right—despite her rather clumsy form, shows some likeness to the 'White Lady' at the same site (e.g. shape of breasts and scarifications). Furthermore, she wears a head-dress identical with that of the figure in white which is painted over her, and this figure belongs to the art-phase of the 'Swimming Woman'.

40   *Aouanrhet: Hippopotamus Hunt. Bovidian Period.*
(95 × 105 cm.)
Detail. The whole painting consists of three hippopotami and
three canoes. The latter seem to be made of some vegetable
material (reeds?) and to be like those appearing on some
Egyptian monuments. Perhaps the vessels had sails. To the
left, under the hippopotamus, a man seated on an ox. The
whole is executed in red ochre.

41   *Ti-n-Tazarift. Our Camp.*
Our camp in a corridor between the rocks as seen from the
heights above.

42   *Ti-n-Tazarift. The Archers. Bovidian Period.*
(65 × 87 cm.)
Fragment of a very fine assemblage representing a fight between two groups of archers. Note that several of the heads
and loin-cloths stand out because they are not painted. The
bows have a triple curve and the manner of drawing them
is that of the steppe populations. One of the warriors is brand-
ishing a curved object which may well be a throwing-knife.
In red ochre.

43 and 44. *Ti-n-Tazarift. The Swimmer and the Archer. 'Round Heads' Period
(Evolved).*
(180 × 155 cm. and 110 × 150 cm.)
Round-headed figures belonging to a huge fresco found in a
shelter. The upper figure (which was at the extreme left)
seems to be moving about in water. There is an indication of
profile and this is rather rare in figures of the 'Round-Head'
type. The profile is distinctly negroid. The head-dress carries
four little very pointed horns. Note the scarifications on the

left shoulder and the chest. The ornament on the right arm seems to be a feather and a similar feature can be observed in No. 22 and in other frescoes of the same style, particularly at Adjefou. These figures, like those in No. 22, wear very heavy bracelets on the left wrist (stone circlets?). However, the bow, instead of being small and forming an arc, is of medium size and of triple curve. One need not suppose that these different sorts of bows always indicate different types of population. Maybe there were two kinds of bows, unless, indeed, that in No. 22 has been simplified by the artist. The figure below has no horn but wears feathers like that in No. 22. The details of the loin-cloth are well rendered as also the motif in the form of a cross painted in the small of the back and which is certainly not a weapon. The two subjects are executed in light yellow ochre with a white outline and belong to the period of the 'Evolved Round Heads'. The little antelope painted over the arm of the upper figure is of later date.

45 *Ti-n-Tazarift. Recumbent Woman. 'Round Heads' Period (Decadent).*
(280 × 108 cm.)
The painting is nearly ten feet from the ground and is in a large shelter whose floor was covered with many faceted balls (hammer-stones?). The picture is in white with a red outline and belongs to the same art-phase as the 'Great Martian God' of Jabbaren. The mouflon, in yellow ochre with white outlines, belong to an earlier phase.

46 *Ti-n-Tazarift. Schematic Cattle. Bovidian Period.*
(230 × 108 cm.)
The legs and heads are foreshortened and thus represent a very special art-style. Likewise, the little figures with animal heads, shown below, have no legs but they are in procession

P

as though taking part in a ritual dance. The geometric, partitioned object is difficult to identify. Inside it can be seen human figures (right-hand side), some of whom seem to be engaged in a frenzied dance while describing an S-like path. The colours are red and yellow ochre and white. The outline design to the right may perhaps represent a stylized ox-head.

47 *Ti-n-Tazarift. The Negro Dancer with bound legs. Pre-Bovidian but undetermined period.*
(23 × 70 cm.)
Detail from a fresco discovered in a large shelter. The tall man with a negroid profile and wearing leg-bands and red and white plumes is the only figure of its kind we found. As there is no over-painting it is impossible to assign a chronological position to this picture. The little figure driving oxen to be seen above is of Bovidian date.

48 *Ti-n-Tazarift. The Dancers. Post-Bovidian Period with Egyptian Influence.*
(150 × 90 cm.)
Fragment. The tall woman on the left is painted in black. Only her loin-cloth and a few details are in red ochre with a white outline. In her general appearance, her proportions and the horns on her head she shows some likeness to the 'White Lady' of Aouanrhet. The other figures (one of which is painted over the woman) are in red and yellow ochre and white. The shape of their bodies, their breasts and their belts shows that they are certainly related to the tall, horned woman. Indeed the whole assemblage must have been the work of the same artists. Furthermore, note the resemblance with the 'Running Men' of Aouanrhet (No. 38)—same head-dress, same rings on the arms and knees, same belted loin-cloth (man to the left). The two frescoes are, without doubt, of the same

period. But we have here works of finer quality as is shown especially by the elegant dancing woman on the right. The mouflon, in yellow ochre with a white outline, is of a later period.

49 *Ti-n-Tazarift. Hippopotamuses. Bovidian Period.*
(165 × 80 cm.)
Fresco in red ochre.

50 *Sefar. The Great God with Suppliant Women. Decadent Period of 'Round Heads'. Photograph of the rock-wall.*
(190 × 250 cm.)
Portion. The whole painting covers thirty square metres. Period of the 'Great Martian God' of Jabbaren. The plate is from a photograph made of the original picture. The antelope painted over the giant is itself surcharged by a motif with a scalloped contour. (*See* the note on colour-plate No. II.)

51 *Sefar. 'Greek Warrior'. Post-Bovidian Period with Egyptian Influence.*
(88 × 183 cm.)
The two figures to be seen in this painting are on the corner of a rock which is not hollowed out. It is this absence of any shelter which explains that the surface has been a good deal disfigured. It was a ticklish task to piece the picture together but well worth doing, since what we found were male counterparts of 'Antinea'. The word 'Greek' (suggested by the crest-like head-dress) is, of course, to be taken in a purely figurative sense. The profile seems of 'European' type, though less markedly so than in the case of 'Antinea'. The head-dress much resembles that of the Jabbaren 'Judges', for on them are found also the same arm ornaments. Likewise, similar colours are employed: greyish-blue, red ochre and white. We

may note, incidentally, that all the paintings of this art-phase are in a poor state of preservation as the pigments have not worn well. Perhaps at the period in question the artists lacked the excellent medium for fixing colours which was certainly used by the painters of other periods if we may judge by the better state of preservation of their works.

52 and 53 *Sefar. The Stylized Negro Masks. Post-Bovidian Period with Egyptian Influence.*
(70 × 50 and 205 × 100 cm.)
No. 52 is from a photograph taken of the mask which occupies the central position in No. 53 (reproduced from our copy). As a matter of fact the term 'Negro' is hardly justified, although there are certain analogies of style between these masks and those still to be met with in Black Africa. All the same, the Sefar masks may be just stylized forms of the head-dresses of the 'Greek Warrior' and the 'Judges' from Jabbaren. There is the forehead band made up of vertical strips in different colours and also the white cap above it, but such resemblances are not enough to determine any precise connection even chronologically. The masks were found in a large shelter overlooking the Oued Sefar and at a few hundred yards from the 'Greek Warrior'.

54 *Sefar. 'Negatives' of Hands. Post-Bovidian Period. Photograph of the Rock-Face.*
(40 × 25 cm.)
We found such hands at Jabbaren, at Ti-n-Tazarift and at Sefar. At Ti-n-Tazarift one of them was placed on the painting of an ox. At Jabbaren another hand was painted over a figure of the 'Judges' type. There are such negatives of hands not only in other parts of the Sahara (e.g. the Jebel Uwenat)

but also in the palaeolithic sites of the Franco-Cantabrian region (e.g. at Gargas in the Pyrenees).

55 *Sefar. The Shelter of the Children. Bovidian Period.*
(50 × 23 cm.)
Fresco painted on the wall of a small hollow in a secondary corridor of the massif. The scene is one of camp life. The line surrounding the figure lying on its back represents a hut. The recumbent man is playing with a child who is jumping on the man's belly. The bow and arrows repose on a sort of table. On the ground can be seen pots and water vessels. In front of the hut two women are sitting with their children by their sides. Farther off a man is milking a cow. This whole fresco is executed in red ochre.

56 *Sefar. The Shelter of the Amazons. Painted Goats and Forearm. Post-Bovidian and Bovidian Periods.*
(88 × 108 cm.)
Detail. This shelter, which is concave in form and fairly deep, contains a very great number of paintings belonging to the most various art-styles. The oldest painting is this forearm and hand. Executed in violaceous ochre, it belongs to the 'evolved' period of the 'Round-Headed Men'. Then comes the animal in the middle outlined in light red ochre. The thing may represent a batrachian or a turtle. There are, in this group of paintings, animals—such as elephants, antelopes and mouflon—but no human figures. The third phase is represented by the man with the long nose typical of the Bovidian style we called 'humoristic'. To a still later phase must be assigned the goats in violaceous red ochre, but they still belong to the Bovidian Period.

57 *Sefar. The Shelter of the 'Street of the Negress'. Archer and Dog. Bovidian Period. Photograph of the Rock-Face.*

(50 × 65 cm.)

Detail. Bovidian painting representing a hunter and his dog. The domestic dog figures very rarely in pictures of this art-phase. The dog in this fresco has a short tail and seems to be less slender than the greyhounds of the 'Equine' Period.

58 *Sefar. Man and Woman Seated. Bovidian Period.*

(285 × 220 cm.)

A masterpiece and one of the finest paintings we found. The profile of the woman (to the left) much resembles that of one of the 'Peul Girls' from Jabbaren. The two paintings are, moreover, of the same epoch. The figure to the right has flowers in the head-dress. The composition represents, it seems, a man speaking to a woman.

59 *Sefar. Men with Tridents. 'Round Heads' Period (Ancient).*

(210 × 150 cm.)

Painting of 'lancers'. It is in the 'Viper's Corridor' at Sefar. Figures with lances (?) or maybe pitchforks (?) whose lower end seems to be fitted with a ball. The figures to the right are of later date. However, the little men in white are also ancient as are also the crosses.

60 *Sefar. Masked Men and Women Dancing. 'Round Heads' Period (Evolved and with Egyptian Influences).*

(87 × 50 cm.)

This fresco is on the wall of a rock which, despite overhang, could never have been used as a dwelling. Only the men among the dancers are masked and also they only wear dance ornaments on their arms and above their knees. Similar ornaments are to be seen in the painting of the 'White Lady' of Aouanrhet which belongs to the same art-phase. The pigments employed are also the same: yellow ochre, white (this latter applied thickly) and, subsidiarily, red ochre. One of the male dancers has, at the end of his arms, long curved objects. The women are neither masked nor do they wear dance ornaments. All the figures seem to be linked together by a cord. To the left (but not visible on the plate) is another little group of figures, one of which holds a trumpet as, again, may be seen in one of the frescoes at Aouanrhet. (*See* List of Styles No. F.)

61 *Tin Abou Teka. War Chariot. Period of the 'Flying Gallop' Chariots.* (80 × 65 cm.)
Two horses, treated in the tradition of the 'Flying Gallop', draw the chariot. The horseman figured above must belong to the same epoch. Chariots and horsemen depicted together are very rare in Saharan paintings and the vehicle shown here is probably of late date. The sketches of men, in 'bi-triangular' style, to be seen on the same surface are still more recent.

62 *Tin Abou Teka. War-Chariot. Period of the 'Flying Gallop' Chariots.* (95 × 63 cm.)
The horses are, for the most part, effaced, but must have been six in number for six reins can be clearly seen in the drivers' hands. The painted chariots of the Tassili have, generally, only two horses. Still two examples of three-horsed vehicles are known, one at Djerat and the other at Tiror. Note that the man to the right of the drivers (and like them attributable to the style of 'Heads in the Form of Sticks') wears a head-dress painted in a different colour from that of the body.

63 *Ala-n-Edoument. War Chariot. Period of the 'Flying Gallop' Chariots.*
    (105 × 73 cm.)

Chariot painted on the wall of a small niche on the track
running from Tekaham-n-Edenen to Ala-n-Edoument. Red
ochre and white. The vehicle is in the 'Flying Gallop' style and
used in hunting (especially mouflon). A discussion has lately
arisen concerning the date and the character of these chariots.
It has been maintained (1) that they are of Roman and not
of Aegeo-Cretan origin; (2) that they are circus and not
war chariots since they never figure in hunting or warlike
scenes; (3) that such vehicles never were driven in the Sahara
but must have been executed from memory by caravan men
who had, in the northern towns, watched the games in the
circus. However, the context in which these chariots appear
makes it clear that they date from a period between the
Bovidian and that of representations of horses shown alone.
Thus the chariots are much anterior to the Roman epoch.
Moreover, despite what has been said, some of the chariots do
figure in warlike scenes (especially in the Oued Djerat) and
the painting reproduced here shows that the chariots served
also in the chase. Furthermore, the utilization of war-chariots
by the ancient populations of the Sahara is proved both by
Egyptian texts of the 18th dynasty and by ancient Greek and
Roman authors. Up to the present time there have been
discovered more than three hundred representations of
chariots in the Sahara—in the Tassili, in the Hoggar, in the
Adrar of the Iforas, in southern Morocco, in south-western
Algeria and in Mauretania. Such a profusion of pictures cannot
be the work of idle caravan men and the representations
tend rather to confirm the employment of this military
vehicle in the most widely separated areas of the Sahara. The
chariot shown here contains three men; the one in the middle

is clad in a white tunic and is about to hurl a javelin at one of the mouflon. To the left, traces of another chariot of which, however, only the wheels are visible.

64 *Adjefou. 'Bi-Triangular' Men. Period of the 'Flying Gallop' Chariots and of Mounted Horses.*
(205 × 140 cm.)
This fresco is on the wall of a rock-shelter which could have served as a dwelling but which contains pictures only of the 'Equine' Period. Above, a group of men in 'bi-triangular' style are marching. On their shoulders they all carry javelins, and these are accompanied by small triangular objects. The oxen are of the same epoch but are executed more coarsely than those of the Bovidian Period. One of the oxen is painted over a two-horsed chariot, and a 'bi-triangular' man, in the same style as those above, covers the second chariot. In our copy the chariots have been moved slightly to the left and nearer to one another. The chariots are of more ancient date than the oxen and the 'bi-triangular' warriors. Note the two archers (apparently contemporary with the chariots), one of whom carries a rectangular shield, a protective implement which did not exist among the Bovidian pastoralists.

65 *Adjefou. The Large Giraffe. Various Periods.*
(105 × 160 cm.)
Painting found in a very small shelter which might, however, have served as a temporary dwelling-place for two or three persons. Six different art-phases can be distinguished: (1) that of the little round-headed figures in light red ochre to be seen between the giraffe's legs; (2) that of figures in the same style but larger, in violaceous ochre, two of which wear

feathers on their heads. These figures are painted over those of (1); (3) that of the filiform figure at the bottom. It is later in date than (1) but it is impossible to say if it fits in, chronologically, between (1) and (2) or whether it comes after (2); (4) that of a round-headed figure in yellow ochre with a red outline. It is painted over a figure of phase (2) and is itself partially obliterated by the legs of the giraffe; (5) that of the giraffe in white with a red-ochre outline. It belongs to the same art-phase as the 'Great Martian God' of Jabbaren; (6) that of the antelopes followed by a hunter armed with a bow. This is of Bovidian date.

66 *Adjefou. Giraffe Hunt. Period of Mounted Horses.*
(85 × 54 cm.)
Small fresco discovered on the cliff-face near a shelter. The giraffe is protecting her young from a dog's attack. The hunter, armed with a plain curved bow, belongs to the art-phase of the 'bi-triangular' men with stick-like heads. Note here a head-dress, painted in red ochre, which may still be distinguished. This scene dates from the 'Equine' Period.

67 *Adjefou. Ostriches and Antelopes. 'Round Heads' Period.*
(160 × 87 cm.)
This painting is in a shallow hollow near a little circle of rocks overhanging the right bank of the Oued Adjefou. The two ostriches are in red ochre. Painted over them is a large feline which itself lies over one of the antelopes. There is, at Jabbaren, a large ostrich, painted in white, of the same style and which belongs, like these figures, no doubt, to the epoch of the 'Great Martian God'. The antelopes, although executed in different colours, are of the same period.

68 *Adjefou. Animal-headed Hunters. Bovidian Period.*
(105 × 51 cm.)
This is a little painting on the wall of a sheltered rock in
a corridor running parallel with the right bank of the Oued
Adjefou. The colours are red ochre and white. Although
animal-headed men are very rare in works of the 'Bovidian'
Period, this picture dates, apparently, from that time.

69 *Ouan Abou. Giraffes Fighting. Bovidian Period.*
(100 × 80 cm.)
The picture is on a ledge overlooking the *wadi*. All the paintings
at this site are of Bovidian age. A circular little wall, obviously
designed for protection (unless it served as a fence), entirely
enclosed the ledge and the entrance to the shelter. Many
arrowheads and flakes (produced in chipping stone implements) lay on the ground in addition to numerous pieces of
pottery. Two of the three giraffes have their legs entangled
as they have when fighting. Probably this picture represents
a struggle between male giraffes for a female (the third animal
shown). Between the giraffes' legs are two gazelles which have
stopped dead in their tracks and (over-painted) an ostrich. In
the foreground is a hunter armed with a bow who is holding
an antelope on a leash and hides behind it so as to approach the
other animals.

70 *The Tassili Barrier in the Region of Tafalelet.*
The Tassili cliffs as seen from the air in the region of Tamrit-
Aroum. To the left a crystalline rocky formation. The gorge
is that of the Aroum Pass.

71 *The Stone 'Forest' in the Region of Tamrit, Ti-n-Bedjadj.*
Air photograph.

72 *The Needles to the North of Sefar.*
'Fairy Pinnacles' seen from the air, to the north of Sefar.

73 *Iherir. The* Kayak *on a* Gelta.
The expedition's *kayak* exploring one of the lakes while the Tuareg look on amused.

74 *Tuareg Family Living in a Rock-Shelter.*
Region of Tin Abou Teka.

75 *Prehistoric Millstone and Pounders. Bovidian Period.*

76 *Neolithic Flint Arrowheads.*
The match gives an idea of the size.

77 to 88 *The Main Art Styles. See* pp. 205–6.

89 *Henri Lhote, Head of the Expedition.*
The dog by his side is a Tuareg *slughi*. These animals do not often take to Europeans. *Slughis* are the formidable watch-dogs of their masters' camps and are used in gazelle and mouflon hunting.

90 to 101 *The Team.*
From left to right. Above: Irène Montandon, Claude Guichard, Jacques Violet, Philippe Letellier. Below: Georges Le Poitevin, Gianni Frassati, Robert Martin, Jack Chambrin. Following page. Above: Jean-Dominique Lajoux, Michel Brézillon. Below: Jean Lesage, André Vila.

ACKNOWLEDGEMENTS

The photographs which illustrate this book were taken by Gérard Franceschi, with the following exceptions: Nos. 1, 2, 3, 4, 5, 6, 7, 8, 9, 10, 11, 16, 17, 19, 41, 50, 52, 54, 57, 73, 74, 75, 76, 89, and the thirteen pictures of members of the expedition were taken by Photos Mission Lhote. Acknowledgements are made to Photos Armée de l'Air for Nos. 70, 71, 72.